What people are sa

Sitting in the Stillness

These remarkable stories bring to life the essence of psychotherapy and the everyday living wisdom of non-duality. The deep wisdom in this book shows us how we can find freedom by fully embracing and ultimately transcending life's challenges.

Martin's practice of non-dual psychotherapy in the National Health Service is unique. His work is an inspirational reminder that however traumatic the personal story, freedom and stillness remain ever-present and undisturbed.

Dr. Peter Fenner, author of *Radiant Mind* and *Natural Awakening*

Explored through the lens of a series of fascinating clinical vignettes, we see how Martin and those he worked with, time and time again, are released from suffocating personal narratives that no longer serve them. Insightful, practically useful, even enlightening, we are led along a less 'self-centred' path with a delightfully light touch. Or, as Martin intriguingly says, 'No longer striving to become a better person but instead realising the perfection we already are.'

Nigel Wellings, author of *Why Can't I Meditate?*

I'm absolutely fascinated by this book. It feels current and necessary to me. I love how much everyday wisdom there is here. The book is wise, peaceful and totally accessible.

Anna Hogarty, Madeleine Milburn Agency

An interesting story of human consciousness written with an intelligent, clear view of our essential nature. An entertaining thought provoking read, the author has created a helpful tool for those seeking to understand the mysterious nature of

consciousness and the oneness of life itself.
J.M. Harrison, Amazon Bestselling Author

We should therefore pay tribute to Martin's work which contributes significantly to dissolving the illusions of the mind, and brings clarity, lucidity and discernment to the daily life of patients, and in fact anyone, who embraces such an approach.
Dr Jean-Marc Mantel, author of *A Scent of Oneness*

Filled with compassion and deep non-dual wisdom, this book is a friendly invitation to the place where therapy, mindfulness and authentic spirituality meet: The present moment, our true home. We are encouraged to be a little less afraid of our own thoughts and feelings, a little more trusting in this strange process called Living. I think this wonderful book will help many people.
Jeff Foster, author of *The Way of Rest* and *The Deepest Acceptance*

Sitting in the Stillness

Freedom from your personal story

Sitting in the Stillness

Freedom from your personal story

Martin Wells

MANTRA
BOOKS

Winchester, UK
Washington, USA

JOHN HUNT PUBLISHING

First published by Mantra Books, 2019
Mantra Books is an imprint of John Hunt Publishing Ltd., No. 3 East Street, Alresford
Hampshire SO24 9EE, UK
office@jhpbooks.com
www.johnhuntpublishing.com
www.mantra-books.net

For distributor details and how to order please visit the 'Ordering' section on our website.

ISBN: 978 1 78904 266 5
978 1 78904 267 2 (ebook)
Library of Congress Control Number: 2019901679

A CIP catalogue record for this book is available from the British Library.

Design: Stuart Davies

UK: Printed and bound by CPI Group (UK) Ltd, Croydon, CR0 4YY
US: Printed and bound by Thomson-Shore, 7300 West Joy Road, Dexter, MI 48130

We operate a distinctive and ethical publishing philosophy in
all areas of our business, from our global network of authors to
production and worldwide distribution.

Contents

Foreword

Martin Wells is a fine example of a psychotherapist who has become aware of the limits of his art and, as a result, the limits of a life perspective bound by past, present, and future time. The awareness of how narrow our conventional understanding is, leads to a questioning of what we are really looking for in life and who we truly are. And so begins a quest which can only end with the full realisation of our authentic being.

The numerous stories of Martin's clients bear witness to the need we all share for peace, love, joy and fulfilment. The drama in all of us is that we look for what we *are* in what we are *not*. So where does this need for security come from? An exploration of this kind leads inevitably to a maturity – to a growing understanding of who we truly are.

Nevertheless, this sort of self-enquiry cannot be accomplished through a troubled mind. It needs silence to mature and resolve itself. By inviting his clients to undertake such an investigation, Martin helps them to reach the understanding that what they are looking for cannot be found *outside* themselves, but only in the *innermost* dimension of their being.

Such a perspective is a real revolution, shifting the gaze *inward* and resulting in a healthy lack of interest in past-future-projections. In this regard, Martin's approach is revolutionary, since it uses the therapeutic process to break the habit of seeking a solution to suffering in the past, opening the intuition to an understanding of a timeless vertical dimension, the source of true healing.

We should therefore pay tribute to Martin's work which contributes significantly to dissolving the illusions of the mind, and brings clarity, lucidity and discernment to the daily life of patients, and in fact anyone, who embraces such an approach.

Discovering who and what we are beyond the dimension of

mind and body is the greatest of all gifts. At the moment that we transcend our ego-driven tendencies, life reveals itself in all its love, truth, and beauty. It is Life which is the true therapist as it guides the mind back to its source. Thank you, Life, and thank you Martin for awakening the essence of being in the hearts of so many people.

Dr Jean-Marc Mantel
Psychiatrist
Founder of the Former International Association of Spiritual Psychiatry
Author of *A Scent of Oneness*

Author's note

The stories in this book are all true. Many have been heavily disguised to protect people's privacy.

Acknowledgements

It is not a cliché to say that without Sue, my wife, this book would not have been written. A heartfelt thank you for all the encouragement, wisdom, patience and brilliant editing. I have loved all the sharing.

A huge thank you to my contributors and for the gift of their stories. Also, for their courage and inspiration. I have learnt so much from them all and it has been a truly joyful collaboration.

A big thank you too to my buddies Vaughn Malcolm and Mark Davies for their friendship and support in the writing of the book. And to Vaughn for all the editing on the road trip to Spain in amongst Joni Mitchell, Bruce Springsteen and Steely Dan.

Admiration and thanks to my Mum Sabine who, at ninety-five, continues to be an inspiration and an example of how facing adversity brings strength, acceptance and wisdom.

Merci beaucoup to Jean-Marc Mantel for inspiring me and so many others to look beyond the world of duality into the realm of love and freedom.

A big thank you to both the late Alice Stevenson and Emily Ruppert, who are very much alive in my heart. They each taught me so much about psychotherapy and being passionate about life.

Thanks to the poets and mystics quoted in the book for finding the words to describe what, for most us, is beyond words.

Thanks to Andrew Clark, friend and colleague, for his generosity, support and the many conversations about spirituality, Christianity, mysticism and cricket.

Thanks to the Mellors, my first meditation teachers, for their support and challenges and wisdom.

Muchas gracias to Adena Frances for her help with the chapter on social dreaming and for co-hosting the groups over the years with sensitivity and courage.

Thanks to John Hunt Publishing for being willing to take the book on and for their support and efficiency.

Part I

Introduction

Malcolm had been sitting in my office for almost two hours as we talked about his suitability for psychotherapy. After he had given me a full account of his life, he looked at me, laughed and said, 'Well that's the story of me but I still don't know who I am!'

Although he laughed, his words came as a shock. This was exactly the same question I had recently been asking myself after twenty years as a psychotherapist. A question that had turned my approach to psychotherapy and mindfulness upside down and made me enquire more deeply into the story of me and my true identity. It was as if I no longer knew who I was either.

How do any of us know who we really are? At one level, of course, we do know! If we are asked for proof of identity, we can produce documents like a passport or a driving licence. We also have our own family history, personality and unique story.

In the few years before I met Malcolm, I had been questioning the story of me, noticing the roles I played, my personality and my personal patterns. Like him I had come to realise that none of these was who I truly am. It was as if I had been wearing a costume. I became curious about who or what I was without the costume, what my true nature was behind the story.

* * *

I was born in London in 1950, five years after the end of the Second World War, to a German mother and an English father. My parents met in Germany after the war. My father was in the forces and my mother a refugee, her home town having been almost completely destroyed by allied bombs and then invaded by Russian soldiers. When my mother arrived in England, she had very little English and a strong accent. So in my early years, I learned very quickly to hide the German half of my identity, especially during war games in the playground! To fit in at all costs, to assimilate into any group. My costume was a chameleon, changing my appearance as needed. Underneath the costume my core belief was that I did not belong; my story was that of an outsider.

Driven by this core belief, I started on a search, albeit unconscious, to belong, be accepted. Over a period of thirty years' training in social work, psychotherapy and meditation I joined teams, groups, therapy communities and meditation networks. I felt part of these and became a senior member of the organisations. At one level I felt accepted ... respected. Along the way I learnt a huge amount about relationships, the mind and how to function in the world. However, nothing seemed to quench a fundamental thirst and the searching continued.

Looking back, I now see that none of this striving could change the core belief or even touch it – nor could any amount of acknowledgement from others. Deep down I thought there was something fundamentally wrong with me and that I needed to search for some way to fix this. I was always trying to become acceptable, a better person, to change the story. For years I followed the well-trodden path of self-improvement, seeking to become someone different.

After many years' commitment to this path, which included workshops, retreats and conferences, I was starting to become increasingly jaded – and was going through the motions. My work as a therapist and meditation teacher was starting to feel formulaic and lifeless.

But one day everything changed!

The words I heard at a conference in London arrived like a clap of thunder, waking me up from my trance. They led me to question what I had taken to be 'me' and to loosen my identification with my story. I discovered I no longer needed to keep searching in this way. The path of self-improvement came to an abrupt end.

Unlike the previous contributors at the conference on Mental Health and Meditation, this speaker, a French psychiatrist, had no PowerPoint presentation, no research statistics or even any notes. His talk was more like a meditation with only a few words punctuating the silence. But each phrase hung tantalisingly in the air for the audience to contemplate. One particular statement shook my firmly held beliefs to the foundations and the aftershocks were to last for years.

The message was simple and liberating.

'You are not your story ... It is a fiction!' said Dr Jean-Marc Mantel ... 'Enquire into who or what you really are.'

The words in themselves were powerful but the quality of stillness in the way they were delivered also made a huge impact on me. Jean-Marc's presence, the words and the silence between the words somehow conveyed that there was nothing to do ... nothing to improve ... stop searching ... just be who you truly are.

At the end of his talk I asked:

'If there's nothing to do and we are caught in our stories how do we find freedom?'

'You cannot find freedom. Freedom is what you are! Enquire into what you are not: not a story, not a role. Strip these away and freedom will be revealed.'

My search stopped that day and everything looked different. It reminded me of the optical illusion where there are either two faces or a vase. No matter how hard you try you cannot see the vase, only the faces. Then one day usually without effort, maybe out of the corner of your eye the vase reveals itself. Once you've seen it you can't not see it.

The impact affected every area of my life. Nothing was the same and yet everything was the same. I could no longer see the world as I had. I can still remember the confusion, the disillusionment, then clarity and relief. I remember a sense of freshness like the air after a storm.

For a while I had lots of regrets and new questions. Why couldn't I have realised this sooner? Why, if there is no path, had I been on one for so long?

I read all I could find about others' experiences, trying to make some sense of mine. Peter Fenner, a colleague of Jean Marc's, wrote that there is a most delightful paradox: that although there is no path to take, we need to take a path to discover this. If we hadn't taken the path, we wouldn't know there wasn't one!

I came across the story of the Indian teacher Papaji. He spoke about how his eighteen-year early morning yoga and meditation practices had come to an abrupt halt. He sought advice and many said he should persist. He travelled across India to see a guru, who asked him how he got there.

'By train,' said Papaji.

'Do you still need the train now that you are here?'

Many ancient teachings say the same thing in different ways. The classic Zen poem makes it very simple:

Nothing to do
Nowhere to go
No one to be
Anon

* * *

Sitting in Stillness is a collection of stories from NHS patients and private clients whom I have had the privilege of working with. They too were searching for freedom, peace, fulfilment. Curiously in the few years after the conference in London many of my clients, like Malcolm, were asking similar questions about their true identity. It was as if they were tuned into my questioning and me into theirs. They too were seeking a shift from a conventional desire for change and self-improvement through to something far more radical: a deep questioning into the validity of their personal story – into what is fact and what is fiction.

The book is not just about individual stories. It is impossible to work with patients in the NHS for over thirty years, hearing hundreds of personal histories, without noticing some strong common themes. For example, so many of us are chasing an illusion of who we think we should be or how life should be. We have become hypnotised, often believing what we are told by parents, advertising, the media and education: that we are not enough, could do better, should have more, all these messages subtly reinforcing the notion that we are not alright as we are ... as though possessions, pleasure and status will satisfy the hunger, bring happiness and ward off depression.

Why do the most prosperous countries in the world have so many people with mental health problems? The Dalai Lama calls the incidence of depression in the Western world an 'epidemic'. Suicide is still the biggest killer of young men in the UK.

But what if we were to turn the usual view of depression on its head?

To see the epidemic in a completely different way. Instead see breakdown as a breakthrough. Where the breakdown can be welcomed as a shattering of personal and cultural illusions and the potential breakthrough of the true self.

Maybe the answer is mirrored in our individual stories and points to the cause of the epidemic – namely that we are searching for something that is already ours.

Seeking ends when the fish understand the folly of searching for the ocean.
The lost writings of Wu Hsin

The stories in the book are from people who, often prompted by some form of breakdown, start to question their personal stories. These are no longer about striving to become a better person but instead realising the perfection that we already are; about ending the search and revealing freedom.

Every psychological crisis involves some form of breakdown. Most breakdowns and crises are frightening and distressing for patients and their families and friends because of the loss of what is familiar and secure. It is a step into the unknown.

What is less obvious is that the breakdown also offers an opportunity. Because of the disruption to normal life, the experience can lead to a deep questioning of everything, which in turn can prompt us to take a step back. The space created is exactly what is needed: it means we can start to closely observe our patterns and personal narratives. We can take our place in the audience of our lives and watch our drama unfold as if in a play. We can then realise there are two 'beings' involved: you the actor and you the observer.

This distinction is potentially liberating as we may begin to see the drama for what it is: merely a fiction that has guided our thoughts and actions. We may still have the thought 'I'm not good enough' but will no longer identify with it and take it as fact. With the realisation 'that's not me' comes a freedom and an enquiry into who or what we truly are. We come home to ourselves.

Chapter 1

The Victim

All the world's a stage, and all the men and women merely players.
William Shakespeare

Janet had suffered with anxiety and depression for over thirty years. She had been treated with tranquillisers, antidepressants and was now having her third course of individual psychotherapy. At her assessment meeting with me she sounded exhausted and hopeless. I remembered her from when I had met her years before and she remained profoundly stuck and powerless.

In her therapy with one of our young psychiatry trainees she had consistently described her husband of forty years as 'thoughtless, insensitive, uncaring' and 'completely caught up in his own world'. She thought that there was nothing she could do about their relationship. She had experienced some major traumas in her childhood. Her mother had suicided when Janet was eight. And she had been sexually abused by her uncle in her early teens.

As a victim of these childhood experiences, she feared vulnerability, had lost trust in others and, as so often happens, this had become the story of her life. Like so many victims of abuse who have been treated like objects she thought of herself as worthless. Unconsciously she expected she would be hurt and further abused. She saw her world as filled with persecutors and her primary persecutor was her husband.

Most of her therapy sessions were about him. The therapist, probably like the husband, became increasingly frustrated:

T: I really feel for her but it's a bit like a broken record. Just the same list of complaints about how awful her husband is …

selfish, thoughtless, obsessed etc.

Many of the discussions in our supervision group centred on how caught she was in her role and how much was projected onto her husband.

The therapist continued to see her each week for over four months. But one week the therapist completely forgot about her session with the patient. This was totally out of character and the therapist was mortified and felt extremely guilty.

T: I can't believe I did that! It's never happened before. And why Janet? Of all people! I can just imagine how easily me not turning up plays into her story. I can just hear her saying:

'Everyone lets me down ... no one cares ... I don't matter.'

I really wanted to give her a different experience. I feel like a failure. That I've let her down. (Looks tearful.)

M: You look upset.

T: Mm ...

M: Lots of us in this field are originally drawn to the work trying to heal our own sense of not being good enough. Most staff and patients will have their own version of this.

Then our so-called mistakes seem to confirm our original beliefs that we're not good enough.

But this is only one way on looking at this ... we could turn this on its head.

T: What do you mean?

M: Maybe these are not failures but opportunities to step back from our stories and see them for what they are.

T: Mmmmn ... Doesn't feel like an opportunity.

M: Well let's maybe think about this from another angle. You forgetting the appointment potentially stimulates both of your stories and deeply held beliefs.

You could see it one of two ways. You could see it as a confirmation ... i.e. 'you're not good enough' or an opportunity to question the truth of the original belief. It's the difference between fact and fiction.

Fact: 'I forgot the appointment.'

Fiction: 'I'm not good enough and for Janet that no one cares about her.'

T: So it's like a replay for us both … but are you saying the replay is a fiction?

M: Yes.

T: I can see that but how could I talk to Janet about this?

M: Maybe start with yourself. You could observe how your story has played out here and rather than see this as a mistake, welcome this as an opportunity to deeply challenge your own core beliefs. This will be a subtle invitation to Janet to do the same.

The conversations that followed between the therapist and Janet about the missed session seemed to enable both to explore how the story might have run its course outside of their awareness and to avoid reenacting each of their personal stories.

A few weeks after the missed session and near the end of nine months' therapy, the patient arrived one day and told her therapist:

'You know I think my husband is largely a creation of my own mind.'

In the supervision group that followed this profound revelation we tried to understand what had happened.

T: How can she suddenly see things so differently?

M: Maybe it's because … after the conversations about the effects of your missed session both you and Janet have taken a step back from each of your stories and started to distinguish between fact and fiction. You've started to see what are 'creations of the mind'.

What the patient had taken to be a concrete reality about who her husband was and (also who she was) dissolved in her new awareness. As soon as she could see the drama and especially her own role in it, how the characters were maintained, she (and her husband) were free. The blinkers had come off, allowing new possibilities, particularly in the way they were with each other.

Three weeks later …

T: There's been an amazing shift in Janet and in her marriage. She and her husband are talking to each other, laughing together, going to the pub regularly and have had their first anniversary celebration for fifteen years.

She's been noticing the part she played in the way things were.

Also, how she has a pattern of undermining her husband, of taking sides with her daughter against him and also of subtly, and not so subtly, excluding him from social events. As a result, conflicts are now getting resolved between the three of them.

* * *

We protect our little fictions
Like it's all we are.
Craig Potter and Guy Garvey, *Elbow* (from the album *Little Fictions*)

When I met with Janet to review the therapy three months after it had ended, she described a freedom and a joy that she could not remember in her life before.

J: I can't quite believe the changes in my life and particularly between me and Pete but am a bit anxious about slipping back.

M: It might feel like slipping back but you've not gone anywhere, just seen something that you hadn't seen before. The good news is you can't **not** see it. You now know how your mind creates stories. There's no going back from this knowing, only the possibility of forgetting.

J: I often fall into the old patterns, though.

M: That's really understandable. The pattern is like a habit that we have repeated thousands of times and has its own momentum. When you turn the wheel on an oil tanker it takes some time for it to change direction. It doesn't mean the wheel isn't turned.

J: It's a bit scary without the old patterns. At least they're familiar!

M: So true! We often cling to the familiarity of our story. We like the security of knowing what happens next even if that involves more suffering. Without the script we don't know what happens next.

J: Also I sort of feel less in control.

M: We like to feel we're in control, particularly when our childhood has felt out of control, unpredictable and full of fear. There is a certain amount of control when we maintain our life position and manipulate others into roles in our personal drama.

J: That reminds me, I spotted an old pattern at work recently.

M: What happened?

J: A colleague told me that the boss was angry with me. I thought: 'What do I normally do now?' In the past I would have gone home, been upset and tearful all evening, taken the next day off sick and come back the following day and avoided the boss in the hope that he would have forgotten. Maybe also punishing him as in, 'now look what you've done to me!'

Without thinking I immediately went to the boss to say:

'I gather you're angry with me.'

He said: 'Yes, I asked you to do something earlier and you didn't do it.'

I said 'I'm really sorry ... I must have misunderstood.'

He said, 'Oh okay, maybe I wasn't clear enough ... in that case I'm sorry too.'

We smiled at each other and the matter was resolved.

When Janet and I thought about this together, she could see that simply noticing her old programme left her free to be open to the present moment. Her old story had been perfectly re-enacted with her boss: with her as a Victim and him as Persecutor. The old pattern would have been to become upset, passive and take the day off, casting her boss in the role of Persecutor, as she had with her husband for most of their marriage. Of course, the whole scenario would have all felt very real, a hologram of her life that would have confirmed once again her story about herself and the world.

What a gift to finally see our dramas for what they are!

If you can see it, you're not it!
Eckhart Tolle

Chapter 2

The Sweetheart – Fear of Freedom

Many years ago when I was still training as a psychotherapist, a book I was reading fell open at a page where there was a story which has stayed with me: Twenty years after the end of the Second World War the occasional Japanese soldier was discovered single handedly defending a remote Pacific island. The Japanese government's response was to send their biggest naval vessel and their most senior ranking military officer. The soldier was treated like a hero, given medals and a ceremonial welcome back in Tokyo.

Only then was he told that the war had ended in 1945 and that what he had been doing for all those years was redundant. The sensitivity to the soldier's potential shame as an analogy in therapy was helpful. So many of my clients were stuck with patterns of defence that were effective in childhood and now, many years later, were redundant. This was also true in my own life and with many of my colleagues. We had found a creative solution to the original problem which now in our adult lives had become the problem!

Dressed in grey, Jim blended into the decor of our NHS consulting room. He spoke quietly with little variation in the tone of his voice and his smile was somewhat plastic.

Jim was in his mid-forties and had been suffering from a low-level depression for as long as he could remember. He had been on antidepressants for many years and with the help of his GP had come off them recently. We had been meeting weekly for two months.

As a child his father was emotionally absent and his mother chronically ill. He had learnt to be a good boy and take care of his mum. As long as he stayed in this role he was needed.

Underneath this his major fear was rejection and abandonment. A fear that, if he were to have his own feelings, his own direction, his own life, he would no longer belong. He heavily defended himself against having any sort of independence.

Part of his defence was to be deeply committed to trying to please the other person. He rarely risked conflict or having an independent view. His mission was to please, often depressing his own vitality and passion, playing the role of 'Sweetheart' as my late therapist, Emily, would call this adaptation.

Jim turned up for his next appointment an hour early. I'd seen him in the waiting area looking agitated. He spoke before he had even sat down.

J: I had a really horrible experience the other night and it has stirred up all sorts of stuff.

M: What happened?

J: I was in the pub with a big group of people I didn't know very well. I'd had a couple of pints and felt very relaxed ... perhaps a bit off guard. Someone brought up the subject of Brexit. Without thinking I blurted out that I thought it was a crap idea and madness to leave Europe. When I stopped my rant and looked around there was no one nodding. In fact, the opposite ... a sea of stony faces! One by one they spat out their disagreement. And it wasn't just an argument it got more and more personal ... and they all joined in!

M: I can imagine how that has really stirred something up in you.

J: Yes, it wasn't just embarrassing ... I was terrified. I know what I was feeling was out of all proportion to what was going on ... but it just felt ... primitive.'

Jim stared blankly out of the window. He gave a slight shiver and began stroking his arms as if trying to comfort himself.

J: I remembered being at school and college and desperately wanting to be part of the in-crowd. I don't think I ever really felt terror like the other night 'cos I never risked standing out. In every group situation I would wait until I knew what the majority view was and then I might say something.

M: I think your use of the word 'primitive' is really powerful. It describes the level of your fear and the origin which was about survival. Hearing about your experience and reaction in the pub reminds me of reading Monty Roberts, the horse whisperer. He observed horses in the wild and noticed that the dominant mare would discipline the foals by subtly excluding them from the herd. The foal quickly learns to fit in in order to survive and not become some predator's lunch.

J: Mmn.

M: I guess that at most other times you're on guard against this happening ... your sentry is always on duty ... ever vigilant. Perhaps, as you say, a couple of beers relaxed you and caught you off guard ... put your 'sentry' to sleep? This vigilance can take a huge amount of mental energy.

J: Well it's true that I've got no energy for anything ... no interest. There aren't any major problems, work's okay, marriage is okay ... kids are doing alright.

I should be happy but I'm not!

M: I also imagine you use a fair bit of energy trying to please others.

J: That's true but even that doesn't work these days. My wife seems impossible to please and is always having a go about something. The kids don't need me any more. They've got their own lives.

My meditation teachers say I should meditate every day but that's only helpful while I'm sitting there and even then, my head can be filled with thoughts. Is there something else I could be doing?

M: Maybe it's more to do with letting go of something rather than adding something else.

J: What do you mean?

M: From what you say, you feared rejection from a really young age. You defended against this by taking care of others and becoming indispensable. This was a creative solution at the time and sort of dealt with the fear. But in another way, it doesn't because you never know whether they are with you because you're needed or because you are simply loved for who you are.

J: I guess deep down I don't think people would love me just for me. I don't know who I'd be if I wasn't taking care of others.

M: So maybe the challenge is letting go of something that has served you so well: it has defended you against your fears, given you a role in life, a purpose and a structure that lets you know exactly how you're going to respond in situations. You might even know in advance the lines you'll speak in your familiar role in the drama. So I could understand why you might not want to let go of the role.

Jim was nodding thoughtfully.

M: Your holding onto your role reminds me of the way my therapist worked; She would help us to identify our particular defences and then she would act them out with each of us in the group, with her playing the role of our defence patterns, vigorously arguing to be kept alive … 'I've kept you safe and secure all these years … you need me!' she would say.

J: I hadn't thought of it as keeping myself safe … but I suppose it has.

M: So it's important then to honour this aspect of you. It really did keep you safe and secure. If you can acknowledge this, then maybe the letting go can follow.

J: Acknowledge this?

M: Yes, acknowledge your creativity in finding a way to manage the fear and the challenge of letting go when this has worked so well for so long.

J: Okay, but which bits should I let go of?

M: Someone once said … 'If you want a little bit of freedom … let go a little bit!'

Jim looked blank and didn't seem to get the irony in this statement.

M: In other words if you want to be free then that means letting go completely of the role that you're trapped in. Unless the role is fully relinquished, perhaps we can't really know freedom?

J: Urgh ... that's doesn't feel at all good. Reminds me that sometimes in meditation it's like there's no one there ... that's really scary!

M: Well, yes. Take away the story, the patterns and the individual ego which are only conditioning and then it's true – in a way there is no one there.

J: It feels like I've been doing it wrong for all these years.

M: No! On the contrary, you found a wonderfully creative solution to your fear. Congratulate yourself! But now maybe you no longer need that solution ... no longer need to desperately keep pleasing others and trying to fit in.

J: Thank you ... but I don't fully understand what you mean.

He said as he headed for the door.

Next meeting – a week later:

J: I had a dream last night. I am on a very long, steep escalator like you have in the London Underground but this one is going through a forest. At first it's pleasant, looking at the trees and plants as I glide slowly by. But the longer this goes on the more frustrating this is. I can see the forest but not experience it. I can't smell it, can't hear it or touch it. I could move if I wanted to but feel stuck to the handrails and to the step I'm standing on. I grow more and more desperate to be in the forest ... to take my shoes off and run ... feel the ground ... the wind in my hair.

The feeling of the dream has really stayed with me. As I was meditating this morning for some reason I started thinking about my work. I'm a middle manager in a large company. The policy is to promote people within the company rather than appoint from outside. There are lots of perks and loyalty is rewarded ...

good pay, low mortgage, company car etc. It's a good place to work but it'd be bloody difficult to leave.

A few years ago, one, my best mate, who is a designer/ engineer, asked me to join him in a business venture. He had a design for a new type of kite. The project was exciting. But I decided it was too risky. His business struggled for a while but did okay in the end and he's made a decent living out of it and travelled the world selling the design.

In my meditation later that morning, I remembered the end of my dream.

Now I'm off the escalator and am running in the forest. I'm naked. There's an intense smell of pine. There are other creatures running, jumping, flying. There's a strong wind. Everything's moving, flowing, connected. I can't control my speed ... more like the running is running me, my breathing ... breathing me.

Eventually I come to a standstill, exhausted. The wind has reached gale force and starts to strip my body to the bone and then the bone to dust that scatters onto the forest floor. I am still conscious and strangely, in the middle of the fear, I feel free.

M: Those are powerful images. What do you make of them?

J: I think the dream image describes my life perfectly! I'm doing the same thing in my marriage and my work ... staying on track ... not taking any risks.

Recently I've been watching my thoughts and actions, as you suggested, and so much of the time I'm trying to please. To work out what the 'rules' are and follow them. It's like an addiction! It makes me feel better at the time and brings some temporary relief but nothing lasting. It's as if I'm only half alive!

M: In Buddhism there is an image of the hungry ghost, who has a tiny mouth and a huge stomach. We can keep on feeding it but it will never be satisfied. As you say, like an addiction we become attached to the temporary relief and the stopping and letting go is a huge challenge for us. As your dream suggests, the identification with the body/mind needs to die for true freedom to be revealed.

J: With all the years of meditation I really think I should have got there by now.

M: That's if there's anywhere to get to! The dream could be reminding you of the possibility of returning to nature ... your true nature. You before the story of you.

In the dream the wind strips away your body and mind leaving a presence and a glimpse of freedom. Freedom from the conditioning of mind and body.

Jim missed his next appointment and I did not hear from him for two weeks. Until I received a letter:

Dear Martin,
I'm sorry. I think I know what needs to happen but it feels too big a step. I feel I've let you down. I've gone back to my GP for some antidepressants which I hope will help.
Thanks very much for your time.
Regards
Jim

Dear Jim,
Thanks for letting me know. You haven't let anyone down and don't need to have any regrets. It takes courage to face what you are facing. You've really clarified something fundamental about your life and your personal story. And you're aware of how much the fear drives your story. This clarity has perhaps highlighted your dilemma and it's making life much more uncomfortable for a while. But I'm sure the next stage will unfold naturally.
You're always welcome to come back to our service.
Regards
Martin

* * *

In some ways I wasn't surprised to get Jim's letter and to hear that he had chosen to go back on medication. Our personal stories provide a familiarity and a form of security. A known set of tracks along which we usually travel. Leaving the tracks means a loss of structure and a step into the unknown. From my own experience this step is not to be underestimated.

Because of my own history of trying to fit in I resonated with Jim's fears and the extent of the challenge that he was faced with. I wondered whether I'd encouraged him to take too big a step before he was ready. Maybe I was forgetting the level of fear that was a feature of my own letting go and that our original fears will almost inevitably be revisited with the same intensity, in the way Jim's were in the pub that night.

Many of us have been in some sort of conflict with our fears and like the Japanese after the war, need to honour the 'soldier' in us and our struggle and look back with dignity and self-compassion.

As Jim says this fear can feel 'primitive' and, as such, is often about emotional survival in the family. There is no shame in continuing to protect ourselves from this fear with our learnt defences. It is perfectly understandable: letting go is a great challenge.

Rest in the shimmering emptiness
That is the source of this world,
And remember who you are.
Lorin Roche, *The Radiance Sutras:112 Gateways to the Yoga of Wonder and Delight*

Without a story we are faced with a blank page, an emptiness. Nothing – no thing. As Jim sometimes experienced in meditation – no one there. This is when the addiction to the role no longer rules our lives. Without the role there is freedom. A freedom of being that is no longer driven by fear and the personal story.

Chapter 3

Superwoman

The cure for the pain is in the pain.
Rumi

As we all sat around the lifeless plastic torso that we were practising on, the trainer for our basic resuscitation training explained what happens when the defibrillator is applied after a heart attack. I was surprised to hear that the powerful electric shock that is given to the patient is designed to **stop** the heart and its quivering fibrillation, after which – all being well! – the heart resets itself into a regular normal beat.

A psychiatrist colleague I have known for many years was a member of a supervision group of consultant psychiatrists. She asked for an individual session that she said was quite urgent and more personal. She looked very different from usual. Like she'd been traumatised … She seemed in a state of shock. Alice was in her mid-forties, an experienced child psychiatrist, married with two children and two stepchildren … she was normally calm and competent: today she seemed fearful, unsettled and confused.

'I think the trigger for what's happening to me has been the difficult family that I've spoken about. I've worked with them for many years, but the parents have become increasingly angry about their daughter's care and the fact that I have not "fixed" her. As you know it's a complicated presentation with high risk behaviours; I've been really struggling to contain the situation.

'Maybe you'll remember when the complaints about my care started, initially to the Trust, then to the local MP, the GMC and to the media. The parents would wait for me in clinic in the morning, refusing to leave until I had seen them. They were aggressive and out of control. I did my usual thing in response to each complaint, preparing increasingly more complex reports. I think I was desperately trying to take the flak and to protect the rest of the team from the assaults. But it didn't work, the family was not playing by the same rules, I was completely floored (maybe I mean flawed). So as all my defences failed, my body started to fail too.

'I've stopped sleeping, I mean, completely stopped sleeping. I feel like I am literally climbing the walls at night. I would often wake my husband in a state of extreme distress. I've become hyper vigilant, quite convinced that my children will be harmed. I'm consumed by anxiety. I feel light headed and nauseous. I've got intense agitation in my legs, often struggling to feel the ground beneath my feet. My appetite is diminished, everything tastes of cardboard. I've lost over a stone in weight and my clothes are hanging off me. Last week half way to work, I stopped the car and started crying. I phoned a colleague, who thought someone had died, I was so distressed. No one had died, but I felt an overwhelming sense of loss.

'My body is collapsing and my mind is following. It feels like a deep raw shame. I've been concealing the fact that I am off work to friends. I just can't talk about it. I avoid people, I hide. I am crying a lot. My children are getting used to me sobbing into my dinner, which only adds to my shame. I am surrounded by a loving, caring family, colleagues and friends. They're all shocked and worried about me. My husband lost his sister to suicide, and my symptoms are not dissimilar to hers. This all adds to my urgency to get better and my shame at falling apart.'

As I listen to Alice the image of the defibrillator comes to my mind. Does the same shock happen to us psychologically? And could the reset be a function of crisis and breakdown? Does the shock to her system offer the potential for nature to reset?

M: That all sounds really challenging and painful. What would be helpful to think about today?

A: I don't know what to do. I've resisted the GP's suggestion of medication or counselling. I find this curious; that in the midst of a full-blown anxiety disorder, a disorder that I've treated many times myself, I am not reaching for a psychiatrist, medication or CBT.

M: Maybe there is a wisdom in your waiting and not acting too soon. There is a story of a ten-year-old boy who used a scalpel to open a chrysalis to liberate the fully formed butterfly within. The butterfly stood on the table for a few seconds, keeled over and died. The boy's grandmother explained that just before the butterfly emerges from the chrysalis it becomes fearful of being trapped, which in turn sets the heart pumping. Blood then is sent to the wings and activates them for flight.

A: Are you saying that I need to let nature run its course?

M: Yes. This could be why you've intuitively held back. It's the much tougher route as it takes you to the source of the problem but it means you're not just treating the symptoms. These crises often take us back to a time when we first developed ways of defending ourselves. These ways were creative solutions to a problem, but in our adult lives have become the problem! So see if you can stay open to what this brings, including taking you back to the origins of your style of coping.

The invitation is for us to embrace the crisis and the breakdown. And stay open to the breakthrough – and the opportunity that it offers.

A: It certainly feels like this isn't just about what's happening now.

M: It's so often a truly creative process. Nature rebalancing. From one point of view you're clearly ready to have these experiences. To revisit the source of your personal story.

A: What do you mean?

M: The breakdown can often mean the exhaustion of a particular style of coping. Whatever is now breaking down is a guide to you to the origins you developed as a coping pattern. It usually comes in the form of a replica of the original problem and in this way a signpost to a time when our personal story began.

At our next meeting Alice told me how she had been piecing some things together.

A: My early experiences were unremarkable. In many ways I had an ideal childhood, brought up in a loving family, the middle of three sisters. My elder sister was an extrovert and straight A student, and led the way. My younger sister, the rebel, suffered from severe eczema as a young child. She would often wake screaming in pain in the night. I remember this, and I remember my mum's exhaustion and sense of failure. I think it was then, that I decided to make myself small and compliant. To make sure that I was no trouble, to make sure that I didn't put any demands on my parents.

I was a deeply sensitive child, exquisitely shy and I clung to my mum and older sister for refuge. The act of subverting my needs would have been quite an ordeal, but I did it and I seemed to do it well. There followed a pattern of relationships in which I perpetually put others' needs first. I remember a deep resentment when I was not looked after in turn. My self-worth eventually became wrapped up in academic success. I began to live my life through targets – once I got this exam, this degree, this placement – only then could I be happy.

Looking back, I think my experience of medical school was deeply traumatising. I was educated through shame and humiliation. I recall surgical ward rounds in which the consultant would not stop until he had made one of the female students cry. Quiet and unsure of myself, I was an easy target. I was filled with shame. No one was allowed to see my vulnerability. I had to get things right.

M: So not surprising that the family you're working with has been a trigger. They seem to have awakened your deepest fears and vulnerabilities. As you say they've broken through your defences. But they also shatter some illusions ... the illusion that you have to always get it right, that you need to protect others and that your needs always come second, that it is shameful to show vulnerability.

A: Mindfulness has helped me see these illusions for what they are ... to find some distance between me and my thoughts. I'm beginning to recognise them for what they are and see the stories they tell.

M: It also means you don't need to identify with the thoughts and the story any more. You can just observe them like a programme that runs.

A: Yes that's true, my parents were visiting recently and were discussing my return to work. They had different opinions, and in a moment of clarity, I realised that their disagreement was often played out inside my head – almost word for word. I began to notice my endless striving for what it was; an attempt to protect myself, to control the uncontrollable and defend myself against life's struggles.

* * *

Alice wrote to me shortly after the end of the few sessions we had:

'It's felt important to write down some of my experiences and record what this time has been about. I feel I am on the road to recovery and now see the light at the end of the tunnel. I've been thinking a lot about the turning point for me. When we first met to talk about all this, I found in you a fearlessness and a belief that the process I was going through needed to be trusted. I did not observe the same fear in your eyes, as I did in others. Your complete trust in the process and your belief that this is an opportunity has allowed my anxiety to settle, initially only for short periods of time. This in turn created a stillness within me. From this stillness, I have been able to explore my feelings, beliefs and values. I became more curious. I've realised that by developing strategies to avoid stress and anxiety, I've inadvertently numbed to all emotions, both positive and negative. I began to recognise that I had continued to use these strategies to keep me safe that were outdated and now unhelpful. I realised that the six-year-old that I was protecting was no longer there. I feel like layers of complexity have been stripped away and I have got in touch with my core sense of self. Even in the depths of despair, I think I realised that this might be a gift.

'Over time, I have found a different way of being. It feels better, it is more authentic and speaks to my integrity and values. It is not easy. A recent bout of ill health sent me straight into weeks of self-pity, disconnection and resistance. In addition, I felt angry and frustrated with myself for not being able to use mindfulness strategies. I realised that there is a risk that I use my new way of being as yet another means of defence. It is difficult to accept that suffering is just a part of life.

'My change is perhaps best illustrated through an example. Recently I was involved in a violent incident at work. A patient physically attacked a member of his family in front of me. I shouted for help, and once everyone was safe, my body began to react. I sobbed, in front of others, a clear display of vulnerability. Desperate to recover, so I could continue to manage the situation, I tried to "pull myself together" with a stern talking to. I caught myself just in time and was able to allow my body to react. I even allowed a sense of gratitude for my body's response which had kept us all safe. With this allowing and some mindful breathing, I recovered quickly, and found a clarity which allowed me to function for the rest of the day. On reflection, I was interested in the fact that I had shown my vulnerability completely without shame. I was confident that I had done the best I could, with the best intentions, I did not ruminate on my decisions in a way that I would have done previously. But the greatest gift, was that because I was not consumed by shame, I was able to look everyone in the eye and thank them wholeheartedly for keeping me safe. I felt connected by the experience, not isolated. Shame does not allow for that, neither does perfectionism. I arrived home feeling tired but not depleted, in fact the opposite, I felt full of gratitude. I recognised my tiredness as tiredness and allowed myself to rest and recover.

'These are all new skills for me, but they are not sophisticated or mature, they are primitive and basic. I feel that I have stripped away layers of stories and myths that I have collected over the years, of who I should be or who I could be and finally I have reached who I am. I recognise my thoughts for what they are. I have begun to recognise my body as an integral part of me, rather than simply a carrier for my head. This allows me to tune into bodily sensations. I am now more able to recognise tiredness, tension, anxiety or even hunger and respond accordingly. I try very hard to be kind to myself. I have developed a daily mindfulness practice and I try to practise gratitude daily. I recognise that living this way requires commitment and, at times will be challenging.

'In writing this, I asked my husband whether he thought I had changed since my "breakdown". He said that he didn't think that I was different, but rather he felt that I was "more me". This resonates with me; I feel more present, more connected and more authentic than I ever have as an adult.'

* * *

The process that Alice describes is not one of attainment or change but as her husband says about being 'more me'. One where the 'layers of stories and myths are stripped away' to reveal what is 'authentic' ... our true nature. Alice's insight into her parents' 'voices' and their ongoing influence in her life and decision making is part of a self-enquiry that enables us to strip away the story and allow what is authentic, the true 'me', to be revealed.

A sculptor was once asked how he sculpted a horse and replied:

'I just took away the bits that weren't horse.'

Alice's role of Superwoman needed to be stripped away so that the authentic super woman could be revealed – paradoxically infinitely more creative and powerful than ego's version. The ego is desperately trying to ward off the thought that 'I'm not good enough' by having to get everything right.

Perhaps perfectionists have intimations of an underlying perfection. Not a perfection where ego is under the illusion that it can do better than Nature but the fundamental perfection in our natural world, a perfect balance and unity without which the planet could not support life. Recognising this, we can stop trying to be perfect and realise we already are part of the perfection of Nature. This of course includes our vulnerability, mortality and humanity.

In the story of the Japanese master gardener the master points to the autumn garden covered with leaves and asks his student to make it perfect. The student diligently picks up every leaf stacking them neatly in bags at the edge of the garden. The master returns and shakes his head, picks up each bag and tips the leaves all over the garden saying 'now it's perfect!'

Nature makes no mistakes.
C.G. Jung

At the time Alice would not have thought of the family that she worked with as perfect, nor the violent incident at work where she felt vulnerable. However, seen through a different lens – that of breakthrough – these experiences are catalysts that perfectly prompted the breakdown and with the second incident, confirm the emergence of the authentic self. Looking back, she could not have designed them better in the service of the breakthrough.

Sky circles

The way of love is not a subtle argument
The door there is devastation
Birds make great sky circles of their freedom
How do they learn that?
They fall and falling, they are given wings.
Rumi

Chapter 4

The Psychopath

Terry was in his late forties, quite stocky with a shaved head.

During most of our first few meetings he would lean forward and stare at me without blinking. He told me many lurid detailed tales of how he had physically hurt people or ways in which he might have. He told me that even in prison he had had the upper hand in the pecking order and been top dog.

Terry had been referred to the psychotherapy service by his GP and the recovery service, as he had become increasingly depressed and lacking in any motivation in life. There was also a strong element of paranoia in his thinking.

He lived with his woman friend, had no children and was not in touch with anyone in his family.

He had had no contact with his father for over twenty years and assured me he would kill him if they ever ran into each other.

His intense gaze and the content of his words left me feeling there was no escape from these images and from the subtle threat and intimidation in the room. I couldn't remember being more scared of a patient. I was thrown back to my early adolescence in North London walking on my own to youth club terrified of coming across a group of Hell's angels or Teddy boys. I would fantasise that, if confronted, I would pretend to be a black belt Karate expert to try to intimidate them. Terry and his gang would have been my worst nightmare.

At aged three, Terry's father hung him out of a second-storey window by his ankles. There followed countless beatings and humiliations. He remembers often wetting himself with fear. He was watching an advert for Barnado's recently and said to his partner 'That was me.' The back of the boy on the screen was completely covered in bruises.

Terry's mother left when he was nine. He has never seen her since. After we had been meeting for six months, he described the impossible choice he was faced with at that time. Go with his mother or stay and protect his younger brothers from his father's violence. For the first time in our meetings he broke down and sobbed. I felt deeply moved and privileged that he shared his vulnerability in this way and by the impossibility of that nine-year-old's choice. My fear of him from the early sessions was dissolving. What was there now was a compassion for the lad who had to learn to protect himself and his brothers.

Soon after this Terry began to address me as 'brother'.

At first I was uncomfortable with this term and in the language of psychotherapy it seemed to be crossing a boundary. It felt too intimate ... there could be a confusion of roles. But as I sat with this, I came to realise that the use of the term 'brother' was a more accurate description of our true connection. A connection beyond roles and titles ... even beyond names. I came to see this not as in family brothers where there is often still hierarchy and story but soul brothers each with a unique narrative. Each seeking freedom from roles and adaptations. Ironically him from the 'bad boy' story and me from 'good boy'.

Having decided to stay with his father, Terry learnt to fight to be top dog. He could beat anyone, carried a machete and a deep sense of justice and injustice. His favourite story is about when he was in his late teens and his father punched him in the mouth. Terry wiped away the blood with a smile that conveyed: 'Is that the best you've got?' His father never hit him again.

The more I sat with him the more I could see the distinction between the tough guy persona and his true self and the more I had the strong sense that this was exactly why he had come. He seemed to need help to dissolve the shame he felt about his vulnerability, to look back with me with compassion and acceptance at this young lad's suffering.

Looking back in this way, Terry began to realise that his way of life and personality was 'only' an adaptation to his feral upbringing. He had done what he needed to in order to survive. But more important, this was not who he truly was.

I saw Terry every three weeks for three years. After about a year of therapy there was less bravado and more warmth. I no longer felt scared in his company but more excited about the discovery of a true gentle-man underneath the bad guy persona.

One day, out in his beloved garden amongst his rare orchids and the bees, he had an epiphany and the thought came to him. 'I love everything and everything loves me ... I remembered a life changing experience years ago when I went into a church and sat at the back. I had loads of questions in my head. The young guy preaching answered every single question as though reading my mind. I went up to him afterwards and felt a deep peace as I realised I was not separate from God. But it's only now that I'm starting to see what this means in my life.'

The eye through which I see God is the same eye through which God sees me; my eye and God's eye are one eye, one seeing, one knowing, one love.
Meister Eckhart

Terry noticed that many aspects of his life started to change spontaneously.

T: Out of the blue yesterday I felt an overwhelming compassion for paedophiles. When I was in prison, I hated those guys and gave them a very hard time!

Also, I now stop by every homeless person and engage them in conversation about how they came to be there. More blokes that I know have started coming to me for advice.

Terry started to think he might make a contribution ... give something back ... perhaps volunteering. I put him in touch with an organisation that helped the homeless and people with addiction and mental health problems. At first he was fearful and pessimistic.

T: After years of homelessness, addiction and prison, I've got no CV.

M: Is that really true?

Terry was offered an interview for a mentoring role with a local voluntary organisation.

M: How did it go?

T: The guy asked me about my background and then said 'you have the perfect CV' and offered me the job. Terry was silent for a while and fixed me with the gaze.

T: You know in one way … I'm not really Terry anymore.

M: No, you no longer need the old Terry. He served you well … protected you … Many people with your history end up in the gutter or in an early grave. And you kept yourself and your younger brothers safe.

But what began as a solution to a problem has become the problem. The defender is no longer needed and now gets in the way of you experiencing love and intimacy. It's really hard to express tenderness wearing boxing gloves.

T: But my ego often says don't let your guard down! Never show weakness … never surrender!

M: Of course. This has served you all your life, protected you. The letting go of the old false self has happened but it can take a while to adjust. A pattern that has been with us for years has a lot of momentum. Unplug the electric fan and it still turns for a while. You now know you are **not** the boxing gloves but the ego does not let go easily. Love and accept this aspect of you too. Let if fall away naturally. Don't give it any energy … then the sap no longer feeds the branch.

At our next meeting:

T: A friend said to me the other day … 'you know what Terry, you're a little bit inspirational!'

I used to need to control others, have them frightened of me. I can still feel that old style and the pressure of it ... But now there's another sort of power. Like the power and intelligence of Nature or God. It's completely different ... much greater than me and my ego. I've been learning to accept the old grumpy Terry as just ego, just ripples on the surface of a pond ... not who I really am.

One day Terry arrived looking a bit shocked and said:

T: My partner happened to search the internet for information about my father. Turns out the bastard died two years ago!

M: I'm sorry to hear that Terry.

T: I'm relieved ... saves me doing it!

Two months later:

T: I can't stop crying ... sometimes for hours.

M: Maybe you're grieving the father you might have had?

At our next session:

T: I'm starting to remember other things about him. How funny he was ... his Donald Duck impersonations. He used to push us round the streets in home-made go karts for hours.

Three weeks later:

T: I noticed how protective I feel towards my partner's grandchildren. When I was sixteen, I left home for a while, slept on the streets. Why didn't dad come and find me, bring me home and protect me?

Terry sobbed for several minutes.

Near the end of our time together Terry shared this story:

T: The other day I invited an acquaintance round for a curry and he brought a friend. The friend was mouthy and loud, and didn't listen to either of us. I told him to quieten down and then eventually to leave. A couple of days later I heard from the acquaintance that the guy had threatened to burn down my house. I couldn't sleep for days because of my rage and an intense need for revenge. I plotted in detail how I might do this ... the thoughts were very violent and reminded me of my life in my twenties and thirties. This was a time of no surrender ... never let someone threaten or get one over on you ... I'm having memories of my father's beatings. I was completely stuck back in the old way!

This time I knew I needed help and asked God for guidance. I heard loud and clear ... 'Let it go!'

All fighting fell away ... I thought I'm finally at peace!

M: I guess because you had decided to never surrender, it meant you could never really surrender ... even to a power greater than yourself.

T: Yes ... I feel grateful for the gift of it all and how the years of fighting have let me know what it really means to surrender.

I also saw myself in this other guy, who is in his sixties ... lonely, paranoid and angry. That could have been me!

I had to have some blood taken the other day. The nurse asked me; 'are you an addict?'

I said, 'Yes, I'm a junkie and a psychopath ... but really I am Love.'

* * *

The psychiatrist and his patient are not so very different ... They are two closely bound friends, who spend some time together and contribute to each other's happiness: that of being heard for the patient in need of love, and that of being respected in need of recognition.

Dr Jean-Marc Mantel

Victims of violence and abuse have invariably been treated like objects. Terry was no exception. As a child, and later by the system, he was rarely related to as a person. He was just a prisoner, a homeless bloke, a patient with a label and a diagnosis.

The therapeutic encounter ideally takes both beyond their roles and labels to an authentic meeting of two beings sharing the same purpose in sitting together. The roles of doctor and patient, well and sick or expert and student can be acknowledged as tools that allow this meeting to take place. The notion 'I come to see you because I'm ill' is seen as a vehicle to lead to a deeper question for both. Why are we in this room together at this point in our lives? The listening, then, is with a different ear. Problems are there not to be fixed but understood. Not another thing to deal with but potential signposts to be welcomed in our discovery of who we truly are.

Terry and I, on the face of it, are very different animals, different histories, CVs and status in the eyes of the cultural norms. But look behind the costumes and the roles and here are two soul brothers. Look behind the mask of the personas and there is the universal. Our differences can be seen as adaptations to our respective upbringings. Both of us 'clay' but appearing on the surface to be different shapes. From this perspective, issues of belonging and separation are no longer relevant ... along with notions of self-improvement, healing and progress.

Self-improvement and healing support the idea that there is something wrong. Terry has not improved himself, he has let go of a lifelong adaptation that appeared to be who he was, revealing his true nature ... loving and peaceful.

If I've helped him it has been by not trying to help or fix him but more by staying curious about the man behind the mask. There never was anything to fix! In fact, in trying to help or fix I assume the role of therapist and invite him into the role of patient. If I can sit still enough, by that I mean, be present without roles and expectations there is a different kind of invitation. From this place we invite the patient into their own stillness, which quite naturally reveals itself as who they are.

Listening to his discovery of his true self has been inspirational and the sharing of his fears and vulnerability profoundly moving. All of this teaching me about love and what it means to be human and to be a man. How acceptance of our powerlessness and vulnerability leads to the dissolving of the need to exert power over others. Reminding me that when fear is faced and embraced it disappears and love is revealed.

Here therapy is a sort of shared wisdom … brother to brother.

The whole frame for therapy changes, no longer the well treating the sick, but love and wisdom seeking and finding themselves beyond the personal.

Chapter 5

The Scapegoat

A couple of years ago I had a phone call from Sarah, a private client that I had first seen over twenty-five years ago. She asked for a few sessions to try and resolve a really difficult issue that had come up at work. As I recalled her story it struck me that I have never worked with anyone who evoked such contrasting feelings in others. As she herself wrote: 'Some people in my professional world tell me I'm a gifted social entrepreneur and others tell me I am a "bad person" with fatal flaws who is always causing trouble.' She was at that time a successful, capable professional: mother of four children; wife of a busy surgeon and doing part time postgraduate studies at the local University. She had been raised in a large family, the third child of seven and one of four girls. Growing up in a fundamentalist Christian household, the split between good and bad was embedded in her history.

Part of the 'family script' … was about the cosmic battle between 'good and evil', between 'God and the Devil', and this dichotomy was played out at many levels in our family and community culture. Physical and mental illness, sexuality, fashion, Shakespeare, television, feelings, the Beatles and much more belonged to the 'dark side', whilst prayer, service and Bible reading belonged to the 'light side'. Normal aspects of life for a lively young girl growing up were 'bad' and a great deal of energy was taken up in 'keeping the dark side' at bay. In our family I became a lightning rod for the 'bad side'. In fact, this was the way in which everyone else was able to avoid their own 'badness' and stay safe on the light side. Rebellion was like the 'sin of witchcraft' and, naturally, I was rebellious. So many things were regarded as 'bad'. When I had bad period pains I would not ask to go home from school, because these too were considered to be evidence of 'badness'. One of the most awful times was when my father cast the devil out of me in the form of a sort of ritual exorcism. I was referred to as 'the black sheep' by everyone, including people in the wider community.

I can still remember the dream Sarah brought me early on in our meetings: It was a nightmare in which a six-year-old girl with blonde pigtails had been run over by a truck on the road outside her home. She was dead. I had invited her to work with the dream and change the outcome – but no, the child was absolutely and completely dead.

Over the next few months, Sarah began to gain insight into the nature of what she described as a 'black hole' and the meaning of her dream. She was able to link this directly to her experience as a young child. She had been raped at the age of six, in a garage behind her home and when she told her mother about it her mother had screamed and run out of the room. The incident was never discussed again. A few weeks later her baby sister died just two days before her birthday, which she shared with another younger sister. As well as identifying with the dead girl she also came to identify with the truck driver – that part of her that killed off the lively young girl who in her family's eyes was 'bad', who, perhaps in her child mind, was raped because of her liveliness and vitality.

When she returned years later, we agreed to meet for six sessions.

S: I know I'm dealing with something with strong echoes from my past.

I'm beginning to experience some very familiar dynamics. I'm being blamed at work for the failure of a system which is itself deeply flawed. And the people responsible for supporting my research and my career aren't doing so. I feel deeply misunderstood and angry. My home and my career are being formally threatened by colleagues who don't understand. In response, I've got some written legal opinions which confirm that I'm sitting on a 'cocktail' of actionable grievances. But after six months of this I'm deeply stressed. Also, my father has developed a paranoid psychotic illness, exacerbated by vascular dementia. His vivid hallucinations are always about sexual abuse. This profoundly disturbed our family dynamics. Although for me, in some ways, it has been a relief that so much that was once hidden was becoming visible. So, it's all happening again and even more intensely this time. Some people in the team are trying to get rid of me and, on top of that, my father's paranoia is stirring all sorts of memories. I thought I'd dealt with all this stuff.

M: I'm sorry to hear what's happening at work and about your father. When we worked together before we were more focussed on trying to find coping strategies and ways to prevent this happening to you again. I'm wondering whether you're starting to face a deeper level of the scapegoat story ... and even ready to let go of the role altogether?

S: I think if I get the right sort of support I might be able to beat them.

M: Who?

S: The people at work who have got it in for me.

M: Maybe this time there could be another sort of winning?

S: What do you mean?

M: I mean freedom. The end of the scapegoat story, of the shame and of your deep belief about yourself as a bad person. If you beat these people would it change this belief?

S: Maybe not!

Session two began with Sarah describing the dream she had the night before.

S: Last night I had this nightmare: I was standing in the foyer of my school – both the one I went to as a child and the one where I was head teacher. I looked up the stairwell and saw a nine-year-old girl with blonde pigtails. As I looked up further, I saw the ceiling beginning to crack. The cracks were opening up and getting bigger, even as I watched, like an earthquake in slow motion. I woke up profoundly terrified. It took me a full half hour to get myself out of the feelings of fear. I woke my partner to comfort me. As I began to rest again and settle back to try and get some sleep, I suddenly had a profound experience of choosing to 'let go'. I thought 'let it fall down' … It came from deep within. Immediately, I was overwhelmed with peacefulness. I fell asleep and woke refreshed the next morning. It was as though the world was a different place. I didn't have to do anything. My whole body felt different. It was like a cleansing and a spiritual reincarnation. It was a sort of 'presence' that I chose to inhabit. Whatever happened in the world, I had this place to be, this ground to stand on, and this story to tell. I know I am deeply loved and loving and, despite everything, I was deeply joyful.

M: Sounds wonderful! I'm reminded of the dream you told me all those years ago. In that dream the child died. This time the child survives! This time the whole structure collapses but the self remains. As though the story of you is a construction and that you've now let the building fall down. What's left is not a construction but the true self … 'loved and loving'.

S: I don't know why I feel the need, after all this time, to talk about when I had the devil cast out of me by my dad when I was thirteen and what that was like.

M: I'm really moved that you can now tell me this. It's as though you have been able to share your deepest shame and the most powerful confirmation of you being a bad person. Perhaps you can say it now because now you know in your heart it's not true and was 'only' a construction.

S: Yes, I think I do know now that it isn't true.

Session three:

S: My worst fear was that without the success and recognition, the structure I had built to protect myself, that people would see the bad person that I really was ... actually it's the opposite. Without the protection and the struggle, I see that there was nothing wrong with me in the first place! I'm fundamentally a good and loving person.

Sarah looked tearful. After a while she said:

S: I have discovered that to let go of these minor triumphs was paradoxically to 'win the war'. But the little victories always left a bitter taste. Letting go of the fight, I felt free. Free from an inner war, from conflict, fear and a need to defend myself.

Several months after our final session Sarah wrote to me:

Looking back nine months later, that February nightmare of the collapse of the building and the letting go was a turning point in every way. My blood pressure returned to normal. I chose not to pursue my usual pattern of an aggressive response to the situation at work but to seek a solution which was the most productive for everyone, including those who had scapegoated me.

* * *

The letting go for Sarah revealed there was nothing to prove and that there never was. What kept on playing out was simply the self-fulfilling prophesy of her core belief that she was a 'bad person'. The other people at her work were mirror images of her own psyche and her original family facing her with what she had taken to be real about herself for almost all her life. The gift, contained in the crisis, is the opportunity to finally discriminate between false and real ... persona and true self ... to awaken from the dream state of the personal narrative. Life seems to provide these opportunities, like Sarah's crisis, and to prompt us to let go, to wake up. For a while the projections from work colleagues towards Sarah and her experience of them became even more intense, as though the 'roof' not only needed to creak and break but completely collapse. Perhaps only then do we realise that the destruction we had feared was unfounded. When we let go and allow the collapse to take place there is a potential revelation of the spacious being that we are.

> Imagine a big building collapsing, some rooms are in ruins, some intact. But can you speak of the space as ruined or intact? It is only the structure that suffered and the people who happened to live in it. Nothing happened to the space itself.
>
> Sri Nasagadarta Maharaja

This letting go is a great challenge for the ego who loves to feel in control. It will have constructed many defences and self-protective strategies over the years. For Sarah, these had worked to some extent and she had even scored some minor triumphs over the people who attacked her.

> When we win it's with small things,
> And the triumph itself makes us small.
> What is extraordinary and eternal
> Does not want to be bent by us.
> Rainer Maria Rilke

In letting go of the fight, Sarah had a profound realisation: if her core belief remains the same the outcome in each new system would also be the same. Before the collapse this view of self appears real and influences all our major decisions and the life we lead.

She also realised that what was unhealed in her childhood could not be put right now. This was her personal hell where all the accolades and qualifications could never heal the original wound or change the underlying core belief.

Sarah's second dream beautifully describes a necessary collapse of the core belief and the old identity. It suggests giving up all attempts at shoring up, or reconstructing. It describes a letting go of defences rather than re-armouring. The dream also encourages Sarah to face her worst fears of annihilation and suggests there is no bypass. We need to go through the crises, not around them. It seems we need to be at our most vulnerable to realise what is not vulnerable.

After the collapse, without the defences and the constructed identity, what we truly are is revealed to us.

'I now know I am truly loved and loving and despite everything, I am deeply joyful'.

The dream and Sarah's response reminded me of the following lines, written by T.S. Eliot in 1942 when he was serving as a fire warden in London at the height of the bombings.

Not known, because not looked for
But heard, half heard in the stillness
Between two waves of the sea
Quick now, here, now, always —
A condition of complete simplicity
(Costing not less then everything)
T.S. Eliot – 'Little Gidding'

If we can embrace the complete collapse of the false self, hidden within each personal narrative, is the source of our being. Another search begins, a universal search for who we are beyond the story. Each of our stories and the challenges they bring offers us a unique key to freedom.

Chapter 6

Peter Pan

David is tall, good looking, charming and very well off. Yet he seems to be cursed in love. I have known him on and off for over twenty years seeing him as a private client. For several years he was in a therapy group that met for a weekend twice a year.

Throughout that time he has been seeking love in his personal life but finding only rejection after rejection from women. The pattern has been remarkably similar. A brief, often passionate, honeymoon period followed fairly quickly by humiliation and rejection. The pattern does not appear in his professional life where he is very successful and creative.

Although David has had many types of therapy over the years nothing has changed this basic pattern. What has emerged more recently is the story of David's birth and his early experience of mothering. Although overtly very fond and proud of him as a boy, his mother was apparently repulsed by him physically, particularly by his masculinity.

He was well cared for as a child and adolescent and almost idolised by his mother, perhaps as compensation for her rejection of him. But this love seemed conditional on him staying a boy and not becoming a man. It was as though no amount of praise or being liked healed this narcissistic injury to his manhood.

During one of our early meetings he told me a dream.

D: In the dream I'm looking at a painting. In the painting a young couple are embracing in a dimly lit street. Looking at them from an upstairs window is an older woman.

Although it's quite a simple scene and seems benign, there's something really disturbing about the feel of it.

M: Can you say more?

D: It's like my mother is present in my relationships, watching

... but there's something sinister about her presence even though she doesn't say or do anything.

I often think the dreams that come early on in therapy can predict the work that is needed and looking back, David's dream was no exception.

In those days, though, I used to think that therapy involved change and personal development. That there was something wrong that needed to be fixed. Looking back, I think this might have reinforced the notion for David of a fundamental flaw, the need for self-improvement and a search for resolution. I no longer think there is a fundamental flaw in our essential being but a fundamental perfection. If we start from a position of something wrong then all our attempts to change will confirm this belief and all our steps to self-improvement are steps away from who we are ... away from our true nature.

For David this took the form of a quest for the perfect partner. Each relationship began with a search for healing but like Tantalus in his own version of Hell, he reached out in hope and expectation, only for the outcome to be the same.

David has often been drawn to women whose own hidden narrative is a hatred of men. Not surprisingly his own secret hatred of women was present but deeply hidden even from himself.

In a group several years ago, David talked innocently about playing with the seven-year-old son of his partner of the time. He described the excitement of the horse play and even an erotic quality to it (not acted out in any way). Because of the context and the histories of some of the group members he attracted a highly critical and aggressive response. Several female members of the group found what he said repulsive as they were reminded of their own abuse histories.

The experience was a deeply hurtful confirmation of his core belief.

Further confirmations in relationships followed each looking different in form and seducing him into a new expectation and a new search for healing. This primal wound or narcissistic injury usually leads to a lengthy and ultimately futile search for resolution. This is because it is informed primarily by a core belief, in this instance, 'I'm repulsive, unlovable'. David's search not only took him on a therapeutic journey but a spiritual path. He travelled the world for many years attending workshops and retreats.

At the end of one silent retreat, David was invited to pair up with a 'buddy' to discuss their experiences. He chose a woman he knew well but has had some conflict with. He touched her lightly on the shoulder at which point she jumped back, waving her arms and shouting 'don't touch me!'

M: What did you feel?

D: I was shocked but not surprised … on some level I think I had expected her reaction … and that I had participated in the outcome by offering my 'contaminated' touch to someone who I knew deep down would react.

The pain of early rejection had been resting in my gut for much of the retreat and I had begun to see that all my clever words were a defence against the primary wound.

M: Maybe the answer is to stop?

D: What do you mean?

M: As long as you're reaching out to the other person, you're not free. You're caught in hope and expectation.

D: So what can I do?

M: There is nothing to do! Each movement carries the same story and unconscious expectation.

Maybe think of your dance lessons. The movements are prompted by the music … your body flowing with a natural harmony and rhythm. In relationship your movements are prompted by your story and a deep sense that you are not lovable and by a fear of rejection.

I am particularly aware during my more recent conversations

with David of how much my approach to psychotherapy and meditation has changed over the years. In the early days I was still searching and wanting to change and would have been encouraging my clients to do the same. Nowadays therapy is to do with a stripping away of false notions of self to reveal our true nature.

M: I'm sorry if I seem to be saying something different from what I might have said in the early years of our working together.

D: Yes, thank you for saying that. I have been aware of this and although it was confusing for a while, I'm fine with this view of things now. I'm starting to realise that I can never find what I'm looking for the old way. I'm even relieved that I might be able stop and have some peace. I'm starting to realise the joy of letting go.

M: I'm glad. Yes, perhaps finally the story can come to an end. The end of attempts to get your mother to love you unconditionally. But it might mean also letting go of the 'special boy' persona. In order to grow up Peter Pan has to give up the capacity for flight. What can then be felt is a sort of special ordinariness.

A few months after this session David's mother died. Although he was able to visit her regularly in hospital, he was not with her when she died, felt that he had let her down and somewhat cheated by this.

D: The death of my actual mother has come at the same time as the mother in my head has been dying off. I'm starting to feel free of a huge burden.

M: Yes, a painful grief and a letting go and at the same time a release. Maybe in some way you've been preparing for your mother's death.

D: I had a dream the other night. I am about nine or ten years old standing in the kitchen at home with my brother and my mother. I have an erection that is clearly visible through my pyjamas but no one says anything as though this is entirely normal and acceptable.

M: The dream seems to be very simple but also profound. A very ordinary scene, where your emerging sexuality is natural and acceptable. Your mother's love no longer conditional on you hiding your masculinity. Maybe it signals the end of your lifelong conflict?

A few weeks later:

D: I haven't mentioned it but I have been going out with someone for a while. It's not passionate or exciting but we get on well and are very fond of each other.

It's more like a friendship, more ordinary, less driven, less intense. We don't have high expectations of each other.

M: I'm struck that you haven't mentioned her. Often when the drama ends we need to learn to enjoy the ordinary. Where not much happens. Peace, stillness and quiet loving connection are not very eventful!

D: I'm going on another silent retreat but not sure what to focus on with these new ideas on life and love.

M: Maybe go without a focus and simply be open to what arises out of the stillness?

At the end of the retreat David had a dream:

D: I am in a fabulous old American clap-board house. There are pets, young people and parents all around. It's so beautiful and welcoming, with old charm – dark furniture, sunlight and old worn carpets.

At last, we are celebrating, for us all. A young woman moves across the carpet and I can hear the soft pad of her feet and see the motes of dust dancing in the light.

We all sit round a polished table of old brown wood, with placemats – graceful yet with a pleasing informality. I say, with some authority: 'It doesn't matter what you do. If you do it with some attention, it will teach you. I don't mean some intellectual understanding, you will find some knowing with your body.'

Watch the dust grains moving in the light by the window.
Their dance is our dance
We rarely hear the inward music but we are all dancing to it
nevertheless.
Rumi

After the retreat at a dance group celebration David experienced
the bliss of moments of complete freedom. 'I was no longer in
the cage.' The dancing was a formalised and acceptable form
of touch but within that allowed the freedom of movement in
harmony with music and his natural body.

D: Near the end of the evening I saw a woman who I'd not
seen there before. She was as tall as me. I asked her to dance ...
the Polka. She was doing her own thing in the dance until, quite
out of character, I said ... 'No it's like this ... you need to look at
me, follow my lead!', she did ... we had two dances which were
fast and exhilarating. Afterwards she said to me 'That's what life
is for!' And left. I have not seen her since and never found out
her name.

* * *

Postscript

This is not only a 'postscript' but in psychological terms what
happens to David, post script ... i.e. when we're no longer
repeating the familiar lines dictated by our stories. In other
words the freedom that is revealed when the personal story no
longer drives our lives and relationships.

D: I was at a psychodrama workshop and an older woman
was telling her story and enacting aspects of it in the group.
She was describing a difficult life and a traumatic past. When
she finished, she demanded a response from the group and
particularly from me. She came over to me and yelled in my face
'I've spilled my guts out for you!' I felt an immense pressure

to placate her but managed to resist ... Though I was really uncomfortable.

M: Sounds like she gave you a powerful invitation into your old pattern?

D: Yes ... I could hear my mother's voice saying something similar 'after all I've done for you ...'.

M: What was the rest of the sentence?

D: Something like 'how could you leave me?' ... meaning grow up and become a man, I think.

M: So as you come to the end of your story and the death of your mother, literally and psychologically this woman's plea tests that freedom ... a freedom from the old script?

D: Yes, the pressure was enormous!

M: But you resisted the pressure to please her or to resist ... even retaliate. You're tearing up the familiar script.

D: A week later I had another invitation. Different but the feelings were similar.

M: What happened?

D: I was at a dance festival and dancing with a French woman but was quite tired and not concentrating on the right moves. My partner slapped my arm saying, 'Non!' I felt the strong pull to fall into the old pattern of shame and rejection but this time just noticed it without a reaction. I allowed her comment to wake me up, adjusted and danced pretty well.

M: Of course we never lose our story but these are two great examples of how you were aware of the potential for the story to be activated in you and simply noticed the invitation, stayed present and free from the tyranny of old patterns. You didn't allow your past to influence the present. This is a sign of the end of the script. The present moment is then a blank page ... unknown.

A couple of weeks later David sent me something he had written:

I come to you now to share a vision of our world made round.

Picture it flat: the horizon receding – say, Westwards – to an unknown future; and the past – say, Eastwards – with darkness rising. Welcome to our round world, the future and the past circled in our hands.

*   *   *

For most of us men the journey from boyhood to manhood is not an easy one. David's challenge in his personal version of Peter Pan has been to let go of a false sense of specialness and come down to earth – to face his core belief of being unlovable which lies underneath the attempts to feel special. To feel the profound disappointment that what he had been looking for can never be found.

Ironically, he finds that the solution is giving up on a solution. The end of the search brings an exhaustion and disillusionment. A realisation that there was no path and that all paths in search of love lead away from who we are. We do not need to seek to be loved. We are Love itself personified.

David has known all along that his struggles were about love and began to write on this theme. The writing flows out of him in the way he has learnt to dance. He can now follow the natural music that animates his body. When the story and the searching end, there is a fundamental stillness. Not a literal stillness as evidenced in the dance. But a willingness to step into the unknown ... to be led by the music not the agitations of the mind. No longer interested in flight but learning how to dance.

At the still point of the turning world.
Neither flesh nor fleshless;
Neither from nor towards;
at the still point, there the dance is.
T.S. Eliot

Chapter 7

The Invisible Man

The crack that rents and
stills a broken heart
Is that which rocks heaven's
doors apart.
Rumi

Everyone in the room seemed to be holding their breath. Paul, a psychiatrist, was describing his history and talking about his two admissions to psychiatric hospital. He had worked on one ward as a psychiatrist and when later admitted as a patient was known to some of his former colleagues.

He and I were talking at a conference of NHS mental health staff on the theme of managing crisis. Paul was describing his own remarkable story of how breakdown led to a profound breakthrough. Of how his breakdown had prompted a painful letting go of the old story and a breaking through of his true nature.

Perhaps some were holding their breath, in touch with their own fear of breakdown. On some level many of us in this work recognise the very fine line between us and our patients. I had heard Paul's story before but each time I was moved to tears hearing what my colleague had been through.

The questions from the audience, when they came, were hesitant and tentative.

Q: What was it like?

P: The two admissions were very different. In the first I was left alone and neglected and in the second cared for in a way that I had never experienced.

Q: Aren't you angry about what's happened to you?

P: No … all these experiences have eventually enabled me to revisit my past and face letting go of the personal story … they have been pointers to freedom. I understood during Martin's mindfulness course that I am **not** my story.

Q: Can we just drop the story and be free?

M: In a way yes, but it seems like to really know the sweet taste of freedom we sometimes need to revisit our personal prison cells and feel with intensity the confinement of those walls.

Paul and I have given several talks along these lines to staff working or training in psychiatry. He says he mostly finds it liberating to recount the story in this way and feels a calling to encourage others in this work to face our deepest fears and vulnerabilities. But I noticed each talk revealed only a fraction of his story.

I had been a colleague and mindfulness mentor, but not having been his therapist, I was curious to know more of his story and touched that he was happy to share it with me.

P: I had an inauspicious start to life: my father's father died the day before I was born.

My earliest memories were of abuse and neglect … with no safe words, no boundaries, no one to hear or witness my cries or screams: feelings of helplessness with no defences or protection at all.

My role was to look after and meet my mother's feelings and needs, to enable her to maintain her collusive relationship with an explosive and frightening man.

My father's extreme intrusion and control, and out of control temper, ruled our family life. He was a caring man who loved us all, but his need to control the fear and anxiety that dominated his life took precedence.

M: How did you cope with this?

P: I came to occupy a sort of 'negative' space … existing to meet my parents' needs or the family's and not really being present at all, as myself, from a very early age. The birth of my sister two years later was the final straw, when I gave up any attempt to be seen or try to get what I needed.

M: What did that feel like?

P: Inside I was desperately alone, isolated and unhappy, cut off from myself and others. I couldn't voice my feelings or experiences. I was acutely aware of being able to be alone and unhappy in any situation. I remember being surrounded by my family and friends on my birthdays, playing the required role of being happy and delighted while, behind the mask, being unable to make contact with others or get out of a bubble; of not really being there at all.

I had also learned to track and anticipate what was happening around me as a strategy to manage and to try and head off my father's terrifying rages with an overdeveloped vigilance, constantly trying to anticipate and make safe the next moment. I thought he would kill me, and my mother.

M: How terrifying!

P: Yes, the fear was always with me and in some ways still is!

M: What about school?

P: I went to boarding school. When they asked if I wanted to go, it was clear to me that this was desired and would please my parents. My clear memory is of having no existence or feelings of my own beyond what was required to do this – of literally not knowing what it would be to have a preference of my own.

I had little or no contact from my family during term time, much less than my peers, and I colluded with this in telling my parents how happy I was and how much I was enjoying it.

M: A powerful pattern had been established.

P: Yes, right through my education. My graduation day is very clear in my mind, I can see the family photo at our celebratory meal, with me strained and suffering, experiencing a migraine … I'm not really there but acting the required role while surrounded by my overjoyed siblings and parents … I'm impotent and unable to say that I don't want to be a doctor.

M: And you chose psychiatry?

P: Yes, I found a home very easily in mental health work where it was much less hierarchical being a doctor and my intuitive understanding – that there was no real 'us' and 'them': that we were all just people – some getting paid, seemed to fit both with patients and staff.

M: But you were still struggling with your own mental health?

P: Yes I was. I sought advice from a friendly senior colleague, a tutor, who shared his own experience with me of having experienced somatic symptoms and of successfully being helped through personal therapy, and through another colleague who sometimes fulfilled a role of helping psychiatrists, I found a therapist.

M: How did that go?

P: I found the therapy terrifying and worked hard to make it safe and manageable by making notes on the conclusions or understanding I had arrived at after each session. My therapist was very humane, caring and accepting and we formed a good alliance, although I found the therapy model itself largely unhelpful.

Two years later, with the help and advice of a psychotherapy colleague, I joined a psychoanalytic therapy group, that met twice weekly. This experience eventually led me into a severe depressive breakdown.

M: Oh, how did that happen?

P: The group mirrored my family. I was not accepted as a new member and the group's problems were projected onto me. I tried to speak about it but was ignored.

My increasing isolation in my personal life reflected both the group process and my internal world. I left the group isolated and bereft and became increasingly depressed.

After trying to manage my depression at home with the help of my GP and psychiatrist, things became too much and a bed was found at a hospital distant from my home and place of work, within the same organisation and where I had worked as a junior doctor briefly several years previously. I was in a bad way and ECT was considered. They didn't seem to know how to deal with me and I was pretty much left alone.

M: And when you came out of hospital ... not surprisingly you were still struggling?

P: Yes, it was an awful time ... I didn't feel in control and feared I might hang myself, with no certainty that I wouldn't. I realised that I was experiencing psychotic symptoms and that I needed to be in hospital. I picked up the phone to the home treatment team who arrived and after a brief discussion found a bed on my local unit and took me in. This was the first safe place I had been (Paul is crying). Almost from the moment I walked through the door I sensed that it was a good place where people could be trusted – a place with a good heart. I think that from this moment, I started very slowly to get better. I was there for a year. I think that this was the first time I had felt safe or thought about in my life.

M: Sounds like acceptance and compassion were the keys?

P: Yes absolutely, and not just on the ward ... the experience of acceptance from my therapist in my sharing of my story in a further five and half years of individual psychotherapy in the years after I left hospital was the most helpful part of our work.

While in hospital, in the stillness of a simple existence, of just getting through the day, and again at home when my focus was on just managing to make some lunch, and that being enough, I became aware of something surfacing in me that felt familiar but barely glimpsed in my conscious memories of childhood – a feeling of connectedness, to myself, to others and the world, and to Nature that was very difficult to put into words.

M: And beyond the sharing of your story came the understanding that we are **not** our stories.

P: Yes, when I came to the mindfulness course I found that the things you, and we, in the training group, talked about, articulated a truth I knew intuitively and had struggled to explain in therapy: a certainty that these learned patterns and defences were 'not me, not who I really am'. In a way this insight or understanding arrived immediately and clearly, because it was something that was already there.

What you said at the time helped by acknowledging the reality of our stories and by pointing out that 'none of this is real', that beyond our stories or what might happen or play out in the realm of form lies our true nature, and it is this rather than the former beliefs about ourselves that is really important or matters in the end.

I understood that our stories have to be fully felt, fully faced and re-experienced before they can be known as **not** who we are. I knew this was what had been missing, and that this was the path that I would follow, home. A home that was there before our stories and that has never gone away, a home for people who have never *truly* had a home.

M: It's a great challenge to stay faithful to our true nature ... in the face of a personal story of wearing a mask and feeling invisible.

It also reminds me of the struggles you've had at work?

P: Yes, not surprisingly the same pattern was there too. I reported some abuses and bullying that were going on but have not felt heard, leaving me with the same sense of powerlessness and invisibility.

M: But you've not backed down.

P: No I felt it was really important to speak about what I saw.

M: Perhaps if we're caught in the original story we want someone to hear us for 'mother' to defend us or 'father' to change his behaviour?

That story comes with the unconscious expectation that you will not be heard and that you are invisible.

What's important now is to speak your truth regardless of whether others can hear it and you have, regardless of the consequences.

P: Yes, it cost me that job in the end ... and more.

Pilgrimage

To inhabit silence in our aloneness is to stop telling the story altogether.
David Whyte

P: Some years ago I'd read a weekend newspaper article about walking the last 100km of the Via Francigena, an ancient pilgrimage route from Canterbury to Rome, which caught my attention, and I'd thought to myself: 'This is the one I really want to do', it seemed to have my name on it, and I had put the article away in a bedside drawer. When a space opened up, I thought: 'this is what I'm supposed to be doing now'.

M: Wow! That's quite a journey!

(When he came back Paul told me about the pilgrimage.)

P: After joining morning prayer at Canterbury, I asked if I could have a blessing for my journey. They offered me a choice of ministers and I picked the one who had welcomed me with a prayer book when I had arrived at the service. He took me out to the recently installed '0km' stone at the entrance to the cathedral and as we chatted I found that he had been born in Malta, to a services family, and I told him about recently having lost my own father. We stood and he said a prayer for my journey and when finished, he put his hand on my shoulder, facing me, and said 'Go well and safely, pilgrim' (Paul cries as he remembers this).

I had been 'named', I turned my back to the church and started walking.

M: It's hardly surprising that having felt invisible and alone for so much of your life you feel 'named'. Not with an individual name but with a universal term for all seekers. A name that implies belonging and the individual search that is needed – to ultimately know there is nothing to search for.

P: Yes, it's amazing – that's what came to me at the end too.

After 1600 miles on foot, I sat down and tried to let it wash over me. A couple of pointers had come to me during an emotional day, reminding me that there were still things left to face and to accept in my story, when I had felt my grief retreating a little, and as I left my pack and walked to the front of the square facing the church hard tears came, not the release I had expected and perhaps hoped for. The words that kept coming were 'such a long way, it's such a long way', not referring to the walk, but to my journey through life and my struggle to survive.

I wrote from Wu Hsin, a Chinese teacher who had been my companion throughout. *Nothing to do, nowhere to get to, no-one to be. When nothing more is refused, the journey is at an end.* I felt its truth powerfully in the writing.

M: Yes, nothing refused and nothing desired or expected.

P: Although in another way, I felt that whatever I had been looking for when I had set out, things were no different now, or any better for me. Giving up entirely, on trying to do anything, I turned, on impulse, into a church I was passing by.

It was, for Rome, a small and poor church, and proved to be deconsecrated but active, with an idiosyncratic collection of shrines and artefacts with information handed out by members of the local volunteer group who maintained it.

I set down my pack, sat and rested, and then, moving to the front, knelt at a pew in front of a large icon of Jesus with arms open, in the orthodox style. I felt myself, in my exhaustion, surrender completely and dissolve and merge with him, flowing into each other and dwelling in a stillness that I did not need to try to hold on to or maintain.

Return – coming home

P: When I met with friends from the meditation group and others, many people congratulated me on my achievement, but in truth, I did not feel that it was something I had done, the journey was something that had come from letting go rather than trying and there was no credit to be taken – the pilgrimage didn't really belong to me.

M: Yes, who is there to take the credit?

P: Although I was in debt, with no source of income, I'd learned to trust the universe and my words and actions seemed to come of themselves – I was no longer the one driving. When challenges or painful experiences or feelings came along, I allowed myself to turn towards them spontaneously, without really trying, welcoming and 'relaxing into' them in acceptance, often finding myself thrown abruptly into bliss, a mixture of peace and pure joy as the identification dissolved – the true background providing relief to the world of form. What needed to happen or be done would happen or be done, I didn't really need to get involved.

M: Exactly, there is really no one involved.

P: In front of the Abbey one evening, where I had attended the Sunday communion service the weekend before setting off, and which had been the real start for me, I felt transparent and empty. I knew that there was a story which would continue to be activated at times and that there would be suffering, or identification with this, but in truth there was no one really there any more. A new relationship came along with opportunities and challenges, reminding me that there was still a way to go for me in acceptance, and my practical circumstances did not get any easier.

M: Life goes on and the patterns of personality remain. Our styles of relating and dealing with the world carry on after these realisations but are now more like a faint line on tracing paper ... no longer the driving force. David Carse calls this aspect of him 'the David thing'. These patterns also have a momentum to them that runs out of steam naturally after a while.

P: The other thing I've noticed is a new level of acceptance. I was in increasing difficulty financially and not having found work I had to face applying for benefits. I think that my acceptance of my situation, and perhaps something of the journey I had taken, communicated itself to the advisor who was humane and kind while dealing with the formal aspects of my application. Leaving the building I started to cry, this was the first person in a position of authority who had treated me honestly or with compassion for some years now and as I sat on a bench and wept freely for the next half hour or so the full distress of how awful this experience had been, and what it had touched, came home to me.

M: And maybe you came home to you?

P: Yes, I do feel at home in myself, perhaps for the first time, starting with the breaking open caused by my illness and the love and care I received on the ward and immediately afterwards. There are only a couple of friends who have stayed by me through all of this. But they're not close by and have busy families and lives themselves. So most of my time is spent on my own ... although this is now a comfortable solitude rather than a painful loneliness.

M: Henri Nouwen said that one of the spiritual journeys we need to take is 'from loneliness to solitude'. Your story has been one of profound loneliness but in the realm of being you've always belonged.

I wonder also if you can acknowledge the courage you've drawn on through all of this?

P: Yes, the cranio-sacral osteopath I went to see asked me a similar thing. It doesn't seem to fit with an understanding of freedom that comes from dis-identification, from ego ... the absence of any person to acknowledge.

M: Maybe because it's not personal. The acknowledgement is of the courage to step beyond the personal, beyond the deepest fears into the unknown ... drawing on a universal wisdom and speaking its truth regardless of the consequences on the personal level. Acknowledgement then is the knowing knowing itself.

* * *

That cleared site is what I
want.
Live in the opening where
there is no door
to hide behind. Be pure
absence.
In that state everything is essential.
Rumi

Paul's is a paradoxical journey from personal and professional invisibility through many attempts to be heard and validated to a different sort of invisibility ... an emptiness: now free of story and no longer seeking recognition. The original traumatic story when fully faced and embraced contains the solution.

The other paradox is that this is not a literal emptiness but a spaciousness filled with love. His family story is either of an absence of love or a love that was controlling and conditional. The love that was revealed in the emptiness is not personal, not of a subject and object but a love finding itself. Love ruthlessly clearing the way for the expression of itself.

Chapter 8

The Broken Hearted

She let go. Without a thought or a word, she let go.
She let go of the fear. She let go of the judgments. She let go
of the confluence of opinions swarming around her head.
She let go of the committee of indecision within her. She let
go of all the 'right' reasons. Wholly and completely, without
hesitation or worry, she just let go ...
Rev. Safire Rose

I first met Jane over twenty years ago when she came to see me
for therapy. She had been seeing a well-known therapist who
had completely forgotten her appointment one day. They had
tried to repair the damage but Jane could not find a way to trust
her again. It was as if something had been broken.

Jane's mother had been depressed during Jane's early years.
She was passive and emotionally unavailable. Jane's father on
the other hand was successful but manic and on the other end
of the spectrum. Jane made an early decision to be like her Dad.
Passivity and inactivity was her worst nightmare.

Jane was a therapist and ran her own business devising
projects to help vulnerable youngsters get out of the difficulties
they were in and find a pathway to their success. She came to see
me with a very specific goal around gaining confidence in public
speaking. Even then I had the sense of something much deeper
calling her to seek help.

Just hearing about her weekly schedule was exhausting, but
she loved the work and was very creative and successful.

I saw her for several years but always had the feeling that
there was a deep well of grief that we could not speak about ...
For Jane to stop and feel sadness seemed too close to depression

and giving up.

Some years later and partly prompted by her love for a man named Duncan, Jane decided to move to South Africa and after a while got back in touch by email.

She wrote:

J: So a few years later I found myself in South Africa volunteering at a children's shelter rescuing the orphans who had to live on the local rubbish dump – and working on a job creation project farming fish in the Karoo desert. Don't ask! It's a much longer story.

I worked for several years literally teaching women to fish and battling with delayed funding, missing money, uncaring officials and deep suspicion from the government departments. (They could not understand why a woman from the UK would be wanting to help the local people.)

Then I had my first heart attack!

And … It was the best thing that ever happened to me.

I lay in the hospital bed, every red light on the monitors was flashing red and my friend, Ann, was looking very worried. 'You've got to hang in there, Jane.' She said. 'We need you.'

My mind flashed back to the years I spent based in the UK, before I came to Africa. They were great years in many ways, working with vulnerable children and adults all over the world and training students to support them better. My 'motto' then was 'let's make a difference to the life of a child today'. But by the end of it I had burnt out. Badly. In fact, I fled to Africa then as the country had captured my heart when I was a youngster. I wanted to find the sanctuary and healing I sensed there so long ago.

I left my demanding role, fled the endless cries of 'we need you!', found my sanctuary – and yet, here I was again in a worse case than before.

Would I never learn?

(Later in another email)

J: All those years of psychotherapy and I was still my own worst enemy! I knew the therapeutic relationships had helped me enormously. I had good insight, could manage my emotions more calmly and my life was considerably smoother than it had been when I swung from one emotional crisis to another. But at some profound level my self-harming behaviour continued.

As the nurse came over to usher Ann away and settle me down, I knew I would have to COMPLETELY change my life. I would have to stop being needed. Stop being passionate about projects that empowered people to live their best lives ... BUT I still want to fulfil my purpose to make a difference before I die. How on earth am I going to do that now?

Do you have any thoughts and can we have some conversations via Skype and email to help me through this?

M: My first thought is that the heart attack takes you to the core of your personal story ... and beyond. To an emptiness and a loneliness that you've managed to successfully keep at bay. Yes, to stop needing to be needed but not to lose your passion ... although this may come from a different source other than satisfying the needs of ego.

(Feb 2013)

J: Hi there. Just jotting down some thoughts at the moment. Still as busy with the project so time is rushing by. My focus for now is on being present and open. Experimenting with letting go of beliefs and having as natural and neutral a response to things as I can manage. All I can do is experiment and notice the current reality which is that I don't do 'now' very well! It has shown me how I have conditioned my mind to forward plan a great deal of the time. I'm also noticing I want to put in a great deal more downtime to my diary.

I have been to see my consultant about my angina attack and feel better generally that I am managing it in conjunction with him and have stopped being quite so scared at night in case I have a heart attack. Suddenly noticed that I kind of let that fear go and left it to an evolving life to take me where I need to be.

Also, I finally got to a place when I fully accepted my anger at Duncan, my lover, for rejecting me and the other strands of emotions connected with him and from that moment on have hardly thought of him at all.

I feel more lonely now than I have before, as I don't have friendships like them here in Africa. But am not fighting the trend this time and not trying to make it different. I like my own company so it isn't so hard to be alone but I would like a bit more friendship than I have. Weirdly I even have had a strong wish to phone my mother over the last week. I think it's about wanting contact with people who care. Not sure where this all fits in with Oneness? Any thoughts?

M: Just a few thoughts in response to yours. When we let go of beliefs there is no need to manage our responses, simply observe them. The deepest layer of the ocean of our being is unaffected by the storm on the surface so we don't need to develop this capacity ... we are it.

This becomes clear when you describe your anger dissolving in acceptance. There is no effort, no position to adopt, simply the natural effect of compassion.

Oneness knows no loneliness. Is a single tree standing in a field lonely? But of course, to the separate ego we do feel lonely ... perhaps this is part of the process that is unfolding for you, again to be welcomed and embraced in its entirety.

(May 2013)

J: I've done a lot of journaling and explored my own actions and drives and found a very angry, empty void (I know that's a contradiction but that's what it feels like) where, out of a deeply held belief in my own inadequacy, I need to impress others and gain admiration and devotion in some way. Where better than a project with very vulnerable and needy people who are crying out to be empowered and get work? Anyway – much debate could go into all that socio-economic-political side!

But the point for me at the moment is that having found that void and seen my sense of inadequacy and internal neediness I felt absolutely fine about it. I felt no need to do what I would have done only a few weeks ago when I would have tried to analyse and work through this as a problem to be fixed.

This time I felt a complete acceptance of my inadequacy and neediness and a complete disinterest in unpicking how I had come to that conclusion about myself. It was just part of what is and no big deal. I felt a great freedom in accepting that part of myself as no big deal at all. It might be true or it might not be true but I had no fear of facing it, whatever was the case. It has been and is just 'there'. This is a big change for me.

M: This is part of a deep self-enquiry, acknowledging our own neediness … especially those of us therapists! The need to be helpful or clever. The need to have a role that has rewards for the ego.

We can come to a place of stillness where we no longer desperately need to fill the void. A beautiful and often painful letting go.

(August 2013)

J: Just staying in touch. Been a very turbulent time physically – and emotionally – as another brush with death has been bringing up all kinds of 'stuff'! Seem to be on two distinct tracks – one to do with Ego being quite clear that it wants to stay here and emerge even more strongly and Spirit being very happy in a vast spacious now. Interesting times! It is deep winter here and I find the cold gives me angina so am being very valetudinarian *(health conscious)* and snuggling up with a mohair blanket round my knees next to the wood burning stove most of the time! I would have laughed if I'd been told I would do this and be very happy doing it a couple of years ago!

M: After all the years of 'doing' the image of you just 'being' is delightful. When we are at peace with our being and enjoying the stillness, ego can take a back seat. Ramana Maharshi said we don't need to destroy ego but that it should be like the moon on a bright summer's day.

(March 2016)

J: The consultant said that I have stabilised well on the new drugs and may well continue to be stable indefinitely as long as I don't challenge my heart through too much stress and anxiety, i.e., no more 'old life' at all! The unknown is whether other areas in the heart will start to disintegrate – which is totally unpredictable, i.e., ... uncontrollable!

I have been continuing with my welcoming and accepting (well, to be honest rather more with my 'welcoming' than my accepting!) and what has emerged is a HUGE superwave of fear which seems to crash over my head at odd times, especially in the early morning, and right alongside that fear, self-hatred and self-disgust in mega doses.

I am staying with all of this and just breathing with it when it happens – sometimes very hard not to distract myself with action – but mostly I stay with it.

Currently the fear and self-loathing are just increasing and increasing – not what is supposed to happen!!! But I am sticking in there. Some memories have come back about the roots of the self-hatred and interestingly, it centred around being made a pariah and shut out from the social community. My mother's words of 'you're too bad to burn' seem to have floated up to my consciousness now.

So, I am starting to live with a more conscious awareness of the loss of belonging as well as the decision to fiercely embrace independence which began with the hospital experience at five years old. This was reinforced by my mother's words and the memories of being about eight years old that are resurfacing. I don't think I have ever spoken about the later memories in all my years of therapy.

M: Glad to hear your news from the consultant and thank you for sharing the memories that are surfacing ... sounds like you are really clearing the whole system and getting to the silt at the bottom of the lake. Remember that self-hatred is still only 'story'. It can feel more real as it has its origins in some of our earliest experiences ... but no more real than any other thought we have about ourselves.

J: I had a very clear revelation that I have no evidence or faith in a God or Force so that I am left with a chaotic, random universe of which I am a part. I have come to accept that my focus has been, is still, and may well remain, on making 'now' better.

Looking back, I think I first wanted to make the 'now' different and a bit easier; then I changed to making it much more comfortable, later to making it happy and then, at the moment, to not making it anything other than what it is and seeing my part in the chaos as being to notice the good and glorious.

These last realisations have been my other learnings after therapy, with which you helped me greatly by showing me ways to transition to another dimension of the self. In an interesting way, having a serious health issue to work with has been an enormously helpful learning and been, in itself, an amazing therapist as it slowed me down enough to attend to this part of my experience.

M: It seems to me that you've allowed your heart to break open, revealing an emptiness that you've spent most of your life defending against. You've had the courage (a word with the same source as 'heart') to face your deepest fear of this nothingness. What's revealed is your spacious being, empty of story ... infinite stillness.

It is only through letting our heart break that we discover something unexpected: the heart cannot actually break, it can only break open.
John Welwood

(August 2018)

J: Hi there!

Thought you might be interested to read this. I'm doing a 3-month online retreat with Adyashanti at the moment. I think I was born to be a nun!

I was particularly interested in his thinking on the dawning of consciousness. Using his framework, psychotherapy becomes a path to inner oriented spirituality. This was certainly my experience with our work. Transactional Analysis kind of teaches us how to discriminate and understand connections and patterns in our lives.

Later he talks about 'repeating the story to someone who is very open etc.' ... this creates greater distance so that (you) have less emotional involvement and actually gain consciousness.

I've found it helpful to see therapy as a spiritual practice in itself.

I could never put my finger on how what we did was different to earlier therapy experiences where the intent was far more on reducing pain and struggle and living a more comfortable life (an easier Life Script).

With our work we seemed (to me) to be placing the process against a background and context of something much larger. In so doing we shifted the emphasis and perspective of the work. No longer about a comfier life, more about a commitment to find out what it feels like to live outside Script and into the vast blue yonder; being brave enough and curious enough to enter that state with openness.

I just wanted to be in touch with this because I have been thinking a lot about our work as I start this retreat. And very much appreciating you for what we did together as I don't think it would have been possible for me without your presence. In retrospect, I think your years of meditation brought the great Unknown into the room and something in me responded to that.

M: Thank you too for these kind comments. Of course, in a way, there is no person to be thanked but a more universal sense of gratitude, no subject, verb and object, just thanking.

* * *

When we are in welcoming, what we welcome is our own welcoming, and we are beyond the mind. The mind is energy, but when we are in the timeless, free from the mind, that is the supreme availability, the supreme equanimity.

Jean Klein

Two days before receiving Jane's last email I was sitting at the screen wondering how to end this chapter. Also, in general, how to describe this type of psychotherapy. Her comparison of the therapy we were first engaged in all those years ago to our conversations now was clarifying and enabled the last part of her story and our work to emerge.

As Jane says, an openness to the unknown allows something else to be known. For this openness to occur there needs to be a breakdown and letting go of the familiar structures; as Jean Klein says we are 'beyond the mind' in equanimity and stillness.

Therapy here is not being done by one person to another. In fact, nothing is being done ... stillness is simply recognising itself. Stillness dramatically reminds Jane to stop and just be ... that being is enough.

Jane's use of the word 'we' suggests the 'work' is truly collaborative, but also with a third party, which she describes as 'the great unknown'. Client and therapist can welcome whatever comes open heartedly.

Even a heart attack is welcomed as an 'amazing therapist' suggesting an intelligence and creativity beyond the mind. We would not choose such events in our conscious mind.

In welcoming we are free from psychological memory, and in being free from psychological memory there is intelligence. This intelligence does not function through reasoning. It is a profound intuition, an insight. It is only this insight that can change the situation, that makes transformation possible.
Jean Klein

With welcoming comes gratitude. For the gift of life and for all of life's gifts in whatever form they come. Life is our therapist. No actual therapist can do better ... this is the grandiosity of the mind.

All that is needed is
someone to explain that
no-one is needed.
Wu Hsin

Chapter 9

The Outsider

The therapy group seemed to have gone well. We had spent the day and the previous evening together exploring how our past traumas influence the way we relate to people day to day. But the last couple of hours went pear-shaped.

One member, Olivia, whilst making some very perceptive observations about the group, had said them in a way that put people's backs up. She had exposed a couple of members of the group by revealing something she had overheard in the one of the breaks. The comments had the effect of alienating her from the others and put her on the outside of the group. As the facilitator I was unsure how to repair the rupture … we were all a bit frustrated and uncomfortable.

Olivia approached me afterwards to say goodbye when the group finished. She looked upset and thoughtful. She said:

'You know I think I'm a little addicted to drama.'

A ripple appeared on the lake in Guangzhou. Most who saw it became interested and forgot about the lake. The world has many distractions, its background has none.

Wu Hsin

The personal drama that played out in the group was the tip of an iceberg … underneath the surface was the story of Olivia's life.

She grew up in an upper-class family in a largely working class area near Edinburgh. As a small child she was looked after by a series of nannies. Although she felt loved by her parents they were very caught in their own problems and as a result seriously neglected her. Her parents also ignored the hatred that

Olivia experienced from her envious older brother. She felt she didn't fit in at home or later at school.

Olivia felt she was cursed by a specialness that came from her family's status at the same time she felt a deep sense of rejection by her family. What she referred to as an addiction to drama was the theme of this story playing out over and over again.

Freud wrote about a compulsion to repeat our stories in this way, as we unconsciously seek a confirmation of our core beliefs. At the heart of this repetition is a search for healing and for a different ending to the story. For example, at the end of the group Olivia orchestrated another experience of rejection.

At the time of the group (over fifteen years ago) I still believed my job was to help people change their stories and, in Olivia's case, find ways to belong. The next few years was to bring a radical change in perspective for me. I discovered that we do not need to learn how to belong but simply be reminded that we do belong … that we are belonging!

The death of her mother a few years after this group ended was earth shattering for Olivia. Her father had died when she was a teenager. The grief was very complex. In some ways she'd never had her mother and now she was gone. Some of the pain and loss was for what might have been.

She turned to her meditation teachers who offered solace and a form of reparenting and later spoke about this with me.

O: It's like a deep yearning. I feel comforted and supported by them but no amount of comfort, advice or meditation really touches it. I feel a little better but …

M: Maybe you're yearning for something that was never lost?

O: What do you mean? Does that mean I should just stop?

M: No, let the yearning exhaust itself. Allow yourself to be disillusioned … like walking towards a mirage.

O: There's already a sense of frustration … That nothing can heal or fix this.

M: Good. This prompts us to really let go. To truly grieve

and at the same time realise that we have always belonged. The yearning you feel with your teachers is a part of this. Let yourself feel it fully, like walking towards the oasis in the desert and also celebrate the disillusionment.

(Three weeks later)

O: I had a dream last night that my meditation teacher had died.

M: What feelings were there?

O: A huge loss but also relief.

M: I wonder if this is symbolic? ... of the death of the guru and the end of the yearning and the searching. The story of the guru is that they will save us, liberate us ... the true liberation is the psychological death of the guru and the end of the search ... as in the book titled *If you meet the Buddha on the road ... Kill him* ... we need to follow the guru for a while to realise there is nothing and no one to follow.

O: I'm going on a silent retreat soon. How do I respond to the leader and his teachings?

M: Maybe let the silence be your teacher. In true silence nothing is needed or sought.

Devotion to any teacher, any sage, perpetuates the illusion of division and separation.
Wu Hsin

(Six weeks later)

O: That old pattern in the workplace is happening again!

M: In what way?

O: I've been asked to act up in a senior role in the school for a while and yesterday I found out that I hadn't been invited to a social event that everyone else in the staff room went to.

M: That really is your old story.

O: How do you mean?

M: Left out but also seen as special. Either way you're on the outside!

O: Oh yes. Each time I think it will be different. I've just started in my new role as head of my department at the school. Getting the special job feels like a victory but actually it isn't. I can see myself taking the high ground and thinking I'm better than these colleagues who are much younger, less experienced and with less training!

M: Perhaps, as you say, there is some addiction to the tension of winning and losing … to being 'special' and different?

O: That reminds me. My first therapist once asked me: 'can you dare to be ordinary?'

(A few weeks later)

O: I've gone back to my old job but into a more traditional role which includes preparing lessons and doing mundane stuff … and because I've not done this stuff for years I need to be taken through an induction by a young newly qualified member of staff.

M: What a gift!

O: What do you mean?

M: What a perfect way for you to challenge your script and life story. Can you be ordinary?

O: It's funny you should say that because I've noticed I'm going into the staff room with less vigilance and paranoia … and not needing to make an impact.

M: My therapist used to say there is a fine line between humility and humiliation. You sound like you are allowing yourself humility without humiliation. Your ego is no longer desperate to defend itself and score the minor victories of feeling special.

Maybe, as one of my colleagues used to say, you can now be the odd one in instead of the odd one out?

O: I feel a huge relief and a letting go as you say that.

(We spend some time in silence.)

I've just realised this is true in the meditation network too.

I'm no longer enthralled by my meditation teachers ... they will never be the parents I was seeking. I can stop striving to be special and to really belong and be an ordinary member!

M: Who always did belong! ... and who was always special in her ordinariness. The need to prove anything to the doubting ego falls away.

(Some months later)

O: I'm really enjoying my new job in a different school. I've been noticing addiction to drama and also a new enjoyment of the ordinary. In this staff group I'm not an expert or over qualified.

I've got a lad in my class who is bit of a misfit. He asked to see me outside of lessons and we just chatted which, I think, just helped him normalise and accept his experience ... we both cried.

M: Sounds like a mutual listening. Maybe you found compassion for your own 'misfit' ... and for the painful experiences you had at school?

A beautiful blurring of who was helping who.

You've been challenging your own 'outsider' story recently and in so doing, realising that you **do** belong. This understanding will have been an invitation to this lad. He will, no doubt, have seen acceptance in your eyes. Two 'outsiders' feeling connected undermines the whole feeling of isolation. This allows you to be different and celebrate that difference without feeling separate.

Many lamps, one light.
Wu Hsin

(Several weeks later).

O: My eldest daughter, Emily, (24) is so angry with me. She says she loves me one moment and then says something hateful. She's been living and working away and having some problems so I bailed her out but when she came back to our place she said

'I hate it here!'

Do you think I need to be firmer with her?

M: I'm wondering whether you need to let her go?

O: What do you mean?

M: It sounds a little like what happens in co-dependency. Of course she loves you but also resents her dependency on you … maybe symbolised by your home. Your home could be a double-edged experience for her … it could represent security but also confinement … like her relationship with you. Time to see her free?

O: For some reason I'm thinking about an eight-year-old lad who joined my class today who seems completely lost … very like I was at that age.

M: Perhaps having children has given you a role and kept those feelings of being lost at bay? You have been talking about Emily and your other daughters moving away from home. Their going will threaten that role and means you may feel really lost again. Emily, particularly, seems to be picking up on your need to be needed … your freedom potentially liberates all of you.

O: I'm realising that what's happening between me and Emily had happened with my meditation teachers. It's a mirror image of what I'm like with them too. The longing for something from them has created dependency and has trapped me … It's also left me resentful … but this is now dissolving.

M: The only thing worth longing for is freedom!

(The following week)

O: Things between Emily and me are easier. It's very subtle. I've not consciously said or done anything different. But perhaps let go of something?

A cousin said she was behaving a bit like my mother used to … ranting and having to be right.

But the other thing I noticed this week is boredom. It's a bit boring without the conflict and the drama.

I do enjoy holidays where there is nothing to do but, as you know, I can even create a drama like I did on one of the silent retreats! I think in the nothingness I start to panic.

M: What's the danger?

O: Being abandoned and feeling lost!

As well as my mother's rants and shouting I'm also remembering her silent treatment. My mother would not speak to me for days as a punishment. Also, she would just go off into Edinburgh to their flat there and not say anything to the family. There was no phone so we didn't know what had happened to her.

M: So it feels dangerous for you to be ignored?

O: Yes ... like neglect ... like being sent to school with holes in my shoes and unwashed ... no one's looking out for me ... it feels dangerous and shameful. Negative recognition is better than being ignored.

M: So maybe you can observe your inclination to get into a fight and stoke the drama. And be one with the boredom and the nothingness ... then stay completely open to the fear that arises ... welcome it.

In the welcoming the fear dissolves and the boredom is seen as a product of the mind ... leaving only the infinite peacefulness of being.

(Two months later)

O: I met with my head today who said how much I'm valued in my new team. I do feel more at peace now in my life but it is ... well ... boring.

M: Thich Naht Hanh once said that if we want peace in our world we need to learn how to enjoy peace. You're faced with the end of your story, the end of the script and the personal drama.

O: Yes, all the girls have gone now and I feel like I don't have a purpose and a role.

M: The end of the story is a great challenge for us ... it's the end of a structure, of a purpose, familiar patterns and the stimulation of the drama.

O: I know and it's not easy. But there are benefits ... like the comments from my head and my relationship with my brother, which is completely different!

M: How's it changing?

O: He's in touch with me every week and genuinely interested in how I'm doing. It's like the old script of how we relate has gone!

M: The ending of your story has invited him into the freedom too.

Now relationships will not be so driven by a fear of loneliness and boredom, in fact not driven by anything. As you become easier with your own solitude there'll be less and less of your personal agenda in your relationships ... just freedom and openness.

O: The end of the story leaves me with a big question ... what now?

M: Yes there's often a strong temptation to fill the gap. So maybe as they say on the London Underground 'Mind the gap!' Welcome the space and don't fill it too soon.

* * *

And to die, which is letting go
of the ground we stand on and cling to every day,
is like the swan when he nervously lets himself down
into the water, which receives him gaily
and which flows joyfully under
and after him, wave after wave.
Rilke

In order not to feel the pain of the core story we find ways to counter it. If we feel useless, we find a role ... if we feel rejected, we find a way to feel special.

The core of Olivia's story is of neglect and abandonment and she has found creative solutions in her work and as a mother to counter this experience. But countering is not freedom, as we are forever keeping the core feelings at bay and forever searching for healing.

Life prompts us to let go but the solutions we found as children to protect us from pain and fear have performed a significant function and we don't relinquish them easily.

In Olivia's letting go she finds a humility and paradoxically a specialness at the same time. At this point she is free from ego's need for acknowledgment or approval.

When she stops striving to belong, a natural belonging finds her in the ordinary loving conversations with her young pupils … a resonance and union that is always present.

The nothingness that is usually part of our experience in meditation is particularly challenging, even terrifying, for those people who have experienced significant neglect. Not being seen or heard was for them truly dangerous. But sitting with this in stillness reveals there never was anything to fear only on the level of form and ego.

All things shall be well, all manner of things shall be well.
T.S. Eliot

Chapter 10

Wordless awakening

You don't go to the Tate gallery and count the brushstrokes!
Dr.Graham Stimpson (consultant NHS psychotherapist
talking about outcome measures in psychotherapy)

Mike was quite unlike any other trainee I had ever supervised.
Most new trainees have questions about what to say to the
patient or what to do. They are usually anxious about this new
situation and feel a sense of responsibility for helping the patient
get better.

Mike was in his early thirties and had been a practising
Buddhist for many years. He was in his first year of a local
psychotherapy training but this was not going well. He was
already feeling it was not for him and the institute was starting
to say that he was not for them. He left the training soon after
starting his placement with us.

The patient we had found for Mike was a single, working-
class man in his late fifties called Brian, who had been depressed
for over ten years with persistent suicidal thoughts. He was
estranged from his ex-wife and two sons and lived alone.

Mike brought his experiences of his meetings with Brian to
the supervision group.

M: It's just such a privilege to be able to sit with Brian and
hear what he struggles with in life. It's painful hearing his story
and I can really hear some echoes in my own life of how men
struggle with intimacy and vulnerability.

In the supervision group each week Mike brought Brian's
story as it unfolded, as he gradually trusted Mike with what was
closest to his heart.

M: I really like him, but I don't think he likes himself.

Mike never asked the question in the supervision group as to how he might help Brian change this view of himself.

(Three months into the six-months therapy)

M: We cried together today about the loss of contact with his family.

Then we shared how shameful it can feel for us men to show their vulnerability.

In the supervision group we talked about acceptance as having the potential to dissolve shame ... and that this acceptance is not a treatment or a strategy but arises naturally when the mind's judgements are observed. Mike's presence, largely free of the influence of ego and its personal needs allowed a space in which Brian could be true to himself and where his shame could be expressed and then seen as the kernel of his personal story.

The therapy ended with Mike and Brian acknowledging how much they had both enjoyed their conversations even though many had been painful. Mike conveyed how rewarding he had found Brian to talk to. The warm goodbye spoke to the level of intimacy shared – and to what brings people together rather than what separates them.

Our normal practice as a service is for the therapist who assessed the patient to review the therapy three months after it ends. So, I met with Brian to talk about his therapy with Mike:

Brian told me that after about three weeks of meeting with Mike he thought 'this is going nowhere' and that the therapy was not what he had expected. He had wanted guidance and advice as to how to change things in his life. At this point he went to see his care co-ordinator wanting to change therapists – this colleague acknowledged Brian's concerns and suggested he give it a bit longer to see what emerged.

Brian told me that something led him to carry on against his better judgement. A few weeks after this he had what he could only describe as 'an awakening'. He said he left one of his sessions and was walking towards his car when all his problems that were normally at the front of his mind seemed to fall away into the background. He told me he had not had a suicidal thought since that time. He also said that one night sitting on his patio looking up at the stars he had lost the sense of himself as a separate individual and felt one with the Universe.

M: Brian, can you remember what was helpful about what Mike said to you in your meetings over the six months?

B: No, I can't remember a single word he said!

* * *

They also serve who only stand and wait.
Shakespeare

Whether we are therapist or friend we can 'help' the other person by simply being truly present. By getting ourselves, our egos, out of the way. By not having a personal agenda ... even to help! This sort of absence of the therapist or friend allows another type of presence ... spacious, unconditional and free.

When we are not tuning in to our own needs or personal story, a natural resonance with the other person emerges. The deep connection that is already present between beings is revealed as is a natural acceptance and compassion.

Mike was not interested in 'doing' therapy but simply being fully present with the patient. As a practising Buddhist he brought a calm acceptance and stillness to his work and invited Brian into his own stillness. We could call this true listening without the listener.

You must only listen. And then, when you really listen, the listening refers to itself. In this listening, there's not a listener, and nothing to listen to. There's only quietness.
Jean Klein

Any words that come when there is no listener have their source in the silent background. Perhaps it does not matter whether Brian can remember any of the content of their conversations because there is another level of wordless communication. The meeting was not role to role, therapist to patient but being to being. Brian clearly felt heard and listened to at this level. There was an awakening of a long forgotten being that existed before any conditioning, before any story.

Words, after speech, reach into the silence.
T.S. Eliot

Brian's suicidal thoughts came to an end too. This happened spontaneously and without effort. Again, acceptance was the key. Often contained in the impulse for suicide is a deep desire for something to end, for an end to the story – a desire for peace and freedom.

As such we can welcome the impulse to be at peace whilst not supporting the suicidal act. There is no need to kill off the body in order to find peace. Peace and freedom are the source of our being and are revealed when there is no longer identification with the conditioned mind.

Brian remained estranged from his family and this was still painful for him. We wondered together, in the supervision group, whether the experience of intimacy and a sense of being rewarding to be with might subtly remind Brian that his presence and capacity for love would, in time, open new possibilities beyond the old story.

* * *

A few weeks after my meeting with Brian, a colleague told me about her recent experience of an equine therapy workshop. Her story somehow reminded me of the quality of meetings between

Mike and Brian.

C: Before we went to join the herd the group facilitator suggested we have a question to take with us. Mine was about relaxation and letting go in relation to my busy life.

We were advised to just join the herd in any way that felt intuitively right.

As I approached the herd, I saw a foal of a few weeks old lying on the grass. It felt right just to lie next to the foal in a similar position.

A few minutes after this, the mare came and stood over us. Initially I was scared. She seemed so big and she could easily have trodden on me or been aggressive in protecting her foal.

But she just stood above us motionless for what must have been at least forty minutes. My initial fear subsided and what followed was the most profound sense of peace and relaxation that I have ever experienced.

Part II

Introduction to Part II

Waves in the Ocean

As I lay on the couch I was a bit puzzled. I had come to see Adam, my osteopath, with a painful knee and he was working on my neck! Had he misheard me?

As though he could read my mind (as well as my body) he said:

'We used to think we had 400 muscles in the body. We now see that there is really only one muscle with 400 pockets.'

The stories in Part I of the book are all, on the face of it, individual stories but they are all stories formed in families, groups and communities, influenced by the group culture and the era in which we are born. We can't really talk about an individual without talking about the system in which he lives. The individual is a 'pocket' in that system, distinct from other members in the system, in the same way we can identify individual muscles in the body … but not separate and acting independently.

We call a tree 'a tree' for the purposes of identification but a tree can only exist as a tree if we also include the earth in which its roots grow, the air and space around it, moisture, light and the birds to pollenate and so on. A tree can only exist as a tree because its roots run deep into the earth on a planet that has an atmosphere and that this planet is a certain distance from the sun and because our moon keeps the earth in balance etc. Everything is connected, everything is one. Meister Eckhart the thirteenth-century Christian mystic once said 'if you could really see a tree you would never need to go to church again'. The same is true of the so-called individual human being as it is of the tree. If we could really see our connection to everything and everyone around us then, perhaps, we might struggle less with what life brings and live in greater harmony with the people in our lives.

In this part of the book the focus is on couples, families and groups and mindfulness. Through this lens the human being can be seen as it really is, not falling into the illusion of individuality and separateness.

The source of all unhappiness is fragmentation.
Breaking the whole into parts,
pitting one against the other,
feeling apart and alone.
No restoration is required.
When it becomes obvious that the fragmentation is erroneous
It loses its power.
Wu Hsin

In some forms of group and family therapy the group or the whole family is seen as the patient ... as one system.

The group analyst is more inclined to say 'there seems to be some anger in the group today' rather than saying 'you seem to be angry today, Bill'. The individuals in the group may then begin to see they are part of a shared system with one person carrying and expressing feelings on behalf of others. The sense of separation and fragmentation starts to dissolve. What appeared to be different realities are now revealed as different perspectives on the same reality. Our minds are more used to seeing the world as separate objects and separate people ... fragments and not the whole. Recognising and accepting this allows us to glimpse the world as it really is ... connected and interdependent.

With this lens, sitting with families, groups or couples can remind us of the interconnectedness of people and of Nature. This is an invitation to the family, group or couple to help them realise their connectedness and dissolve the sense of isolation and aloneness.

The word 'alone' derives from 'all one'. How else would I
come to know that I am one with nature, the river, and the
Tao without experiencing it.
David Rosen

We don't need to ignore differences but simply realise that
everything in Nature has the same source. The lion and the
domestic cat are from the same family but lead very different
lives. The rose and the lily have different colourings and
fragrances but are rooted and grow in the same earth and share
the same light.

This interconnectedness is borne out in the world of science
and quantum physics. The more closely we have looked at
the make-up of our world the more the connections between
everything have become apparent. In the same way, if we closely
observe what happens in families and in groups we see past the
collection of individuals to an intimately connected and self-
regulating system. Spend some time holding your partner and
you will notice that your breathing assumes the same rhythm.
Women who live together for a while often fall into the same
menstrual pattern.

We say that inseparable quantum interconnectedness of the
whole universe is the fundamental reality, and that relatively
independently behaving parts are merely particular and
contingent forms within this whole.
David Bohm

When the psychoanalyst S.F. Foulkes decided to see some of
his individual patients in a group his colleagues were horrified.
They were more focussed on the individual struggles with
dependency not appreciating that in nature there is no true
independence. Foulkes, who went on to found group analysis,
said that in reality there was no such thing as an individual. All

of us are products of the groups we grow up in and the context in which we live.

However, just as in the individual stories, our freedom lies beyond these influences. Ultimately, we are not our stories, our families or our culture. In the same way as we might observe the 'individual' mind, the influences of the group can be enquired into and observed with acceptance and compassion. The essence of mindfulness in therapy is to fully accept these influences and the powerful hold they have over us and to realise that fundamentally our true nature is **not** the product of the groups we grew up in or now live in. When these are seen instead as merely conditioning then their influence dissolves revealing glimpses of the true self ... the unconditioned mind.

The full acceptance of our interdependence and the influence of these systems means we can loosen our grip on the illusion that our ego is in charge. We might begin to let go of our attempts to control what is beyond our control. This includes letting go of our personal goals. This letting go is a great challenge, particularly for the ego, but it brings an openness to going with the flow of life as it is. It brings a different sort of freedom and a different sort of power.

Personal freedom is nothing more than freedom from the personal.
Wu Hsin

Chapter 11

Couples Therapy: It Takes Two to Tango

I just want you to hurt like I do.
Randy Newman

The tip if the iceberg for Jill and Nick was their squabbles about money and how to manage it. They told me they had been talking about divorce, so clearly something more serious was beneath the surface.

Nick: Every bank statement seems to be red at the moment and when we talk about it, it leads to a fight.

Jill: Yeah, five hundred pounds overdrawn, I reckon that's serious! We need to do something and soon. I'm really worried.

N: You worry too much. It'll all be fine. I'm getting paid soon.

J: You're too slack and laid back about it all. How's it going to change if we don't do something?

N: And you're too anxious about it, always trying to control things.

Each version of these conversations ended in frustration, each of them focussed on their differences and thinking that the other needed to change.

As the therapist I felt stuck too …. caught in the middle. I had a conversation with my meditation teacher at the time.

K: Maybe see them as one organism, naturally in balance but each taking polarised positions to maintain that balance.

This perspective enabled me to see union rather than division and some different words came when I was next with them.

M: I had an image of you both on a seesaw maintaining a balance but a long way apart. Somewhere in the middle of your two positions seems to be appropriate given your financial situation. In other words, it will be alright **and** you need to take some action.

N: She can if she likes but I don't want to be bothered with it … there's more important things to worry about.

J: That's what you always say … nothing will ever change!

N: There we go … same old stuff. How do we get past this?

(J could not make our next session so I saw N on his own)

M: I'm glad of this opportunity to think about this with you.

N: Why?

M: I was thinking about your question last time about how you get past what you're both stuck with.

At the moment you and Jill are maintaining the balance in your marriage by being poles apart. The balance on a seesaw is maintained when you get closer to each other's position … so I suggest you not only get closer to Jill's position but adopt it fully.

N: Well okay, but I don't think that will be easy.

M: No, probably not … but in a way that's the point. You're letting her carry the aspect of this that you're not comfortable with. You don't like to see yourself as controlling or in any way uptight … that would disturb your view of yourself as chilled.

(Next session)

N: What you suggested I do last time was very uncomfortable at first but ultimately liberating. I didn't like to see myself as worried or controlling but started to see that I was happy to let Jill carry this role. Biting the bullet, I was able to own that these qualities were me too … just well hidden.

The next time the bank statement came through the post it was red again. But this time I could feel some anxiety about it and said: 'I'm really concerned about being overdrawn and think we should do something!'

J: And I said without thinking … 'No don't worry it'll be okay' (she laughed).

N: Amazing! I hadn't spoken about this to Jill before this conversation. How could this happen?

M: Look at the natural world ... everything is in balance. You were maintaining a balance in your marriage but did so by being a long way apart. It doesn't matter who takes up which position ... balance is restored.

Even more important, this can highlight what a perfect choice you've made in each other.

J: How?

M: It's an opportunity to become a whole person ... to reclaim the parts we're uncomfortable with, that we let the other carry.

(Next session)

N: I think what we came to you with is just the tip of the iceberg.

M: Yes, I can imagine that. Often, we need to start with what's visible to go deeper. What are you noticing?

N: Funnily enough, now that we're not fighting so much I'm starting to feel afraid.

M: Of?

N: That Jill will leave me.

M: Can you say some more?

N: Well ... it's not easy to say ... but she really understands me ... I need her ... but I'm afraid too much ... like I'm too much!

M: And you Jill?

J: Yeah, for me I feel sort of smothered by Nick ... like I can't breathe!

We did split up for a while once before but that wasn't right either.

M: Our close relationships inevitably stimulate our earliest attachments. I suggest you don't avoid these fears but fully embrace them and see what emerges.

(Next session)

J: The more I went into my fear, the more painful that got. I had images of my mum and her drinking ... of having to look after her whether she was drunk or sober. She actually fell asleep on top of me once!

I think when I get a whiff of Nick's neediness this all gets stirred up ... and to be honest, I need to push him away!

N: And when I sense that I get really scared of rejection. My mother left when I was three ... I guess that's in there somewhere?

M: Most of us have a primary fear of abandonment or engulfment.

J: How do you mean?

M: Nick's neediness, as you call it, could well trigger memories of you feeling overwhelmed and engulfed by your mother.

These fears are rooted in early attachment patterns. So, no surprise it takes you both back to your first attachments.

Also couples often get together with someone with the complementary fear. Each unconsciously seeking reunion with split off parts of themselves ... As with you two each triggering in the other an early attachment issue that is unresolved as though we know what and who is needed to restore wholeness ... it's very creative.

N: It doesn't feel creative!

M: Agreed. But if we're to revisit the original fear who better than someone we love to take us there.

J: But why do we need to go there at all?

M: Because your fears get in the way of true intimacy. I'm not suggesting you can just be rid of them. The creative potential is that you face each other with the possibility of a deep acceptance of these fears in a way that wasn't possible when you were infants.

At that age the fear might well have been for your very survival!

Now you can face these fears knowing that your survival is no longer at stake. More than this you can even acknowledge that you were seeking love and union ... only your mothers' stories got in the way, which you took personally ... often some version of 'there's something wrong with me'.

N: Where do we go from here?

M: Nowhere really. You're already doing what needs to be done, finding each other, stirring up your past, feeling the fear and sitting here. The fact that we're having this conversation means you're ready to accept and even welcome these fears in all their intensity.

Just stay open to what gets stirred up between you. Observe any judgements you make or any evaluations of good and bad.

Again, trust the natural balance in Nature ... in you ... and an intelligence that lies well beyond the mind. All this is unfolding anyway ... you may as well enjoy the ride!

(Next session – two weeks later)

N: I think we both got what you were talking about last time, it felt right ... but things are getting worse and we're still talking about breaking up!

M: Don't confuse something that needs to break up between you and separating. Marriage is a bit like a reptile ... from time to time it needs to lose a skin in order to grow. The old skin breaks up and this usually involves some vigorous process of shedding. The growth of the new skin has forced off the old. At this time the reptile is at its most vulnerable to predators.

As couples we harden our skins with each other and often cling on to the structure for fear of the vulnerability underneath. Again, notice the creativity here ... the breaking up is part of the growth. But many couples confuse this process with the need to break up. That doesn't mean that couples should never break up ... only that done too soon might mean the loss of a golden opportunity to face and let go of the fears of the past.

(Next session – two weeks later)

N: This whole thing is really tough ... like quicksand ... not getting anywhere just going in deeper.

M: Yes, sure ... it's like your personal hell. Partly because you're seeking something that can no longer be found ... you can't change what happened with your mum.

N: But if I stop trying to change things, it feels like giving up.

M: Yes ... give up!

Nick looks like this suggestion has completely taken the wind out of his sails ... he becomes still and looks younger, childlike ... and after a while starts to sob quietly.

M: Let it go ... you're grieving for what was not and can never be ... at least in that way. The grief sets you both free. This way you're no longer needing Jill to put it right ... it takes a huge and impossible burden off her. It also means that she no longer has to defend herself against your neediness by pushing you away.

You can then be with each other in the present ... with the real person and not some projection from your past.

N: But it's like there's no hope anymore.

M: That's a part of the grief ... welcome that too. It's all in the service of your freedom.

* * *

Identification with your mind creates an opaque screen of objects, labels, images, words, judgements and definitions that blocks all true relationship. It comes between you and yourself, between you and your fellow man and woman, between you and nature, between you and God. It is this screen of thought that creates the illusion of separateness, the illusion that there is you and a totally separate 'other'. You then forget the essential fact that, underneath the level of physical appearances and separate forms, you are one with all that is.

Eckhart Tolle

Like many couples Nick and Jill were relating to each other as separate objects having 'chosen' the other in pursuit of happiness. As Tolle also says 'The same person who made me happy now makes me unhappy!' This is a common view in our culture. Individuals looking for Mr or Mrs Right ... so why is it that so often Mr Right ends up looking like Mr Wrong.

As Tolle says, we are hypnotised by a world of 'physical appearances and separate forms'. Change the lens and it's clear that everything is connected.

Then looking beyond the superficial choice of another object/person is oneness manifesting, which brings a radically different perspective on what it means to be in relationship with someone else. With this lens, oneness seeks itself and like Nick and Jill each brings the other the aspect of themselves they have split off from.

The original attachment trauma created a fragmentation, an inner splitting and a story to go with it. For example, for Nick this was a sense of being too much, with a deep fear and expectation of rejection. For Jill, a fear of being, of not having enough space, of being overwhelmed. Jill and Nick perfectly mirrored these parts to each other stimulating the original fear. In our normal superficial frame things were going wrong and maybe they should find a 'better' partner.

With oneness in view, what could be better than each partner bringing the other the perfect opportunity to realise their wholeness? Stimulating an old fear that can now dissolve in the loving attention of the heart.

Chapter 12

Family Therapy – One Train Hides Another

At level crossings in France there is often a cautionary sign which says *Un train peut cache un autre*. Meaning one train hides another. In working with families, it is helpful to wonder what is hidden behind the presenting problem.

In the film 'Lars and the Real Girl', Lars is a loner and lives at the bottom of his brother and sister-in-law's garden, orders a life-like doll off the internet and passes her off as his girlfriend, Bianca. The brother and sister-in-law go to the local GP saying that Lars seems to have lost it and wondering if he's psychotic. The doctor takes a different view and recommends patience saying 'I think that maybe Bianca is in town for a reason!'

Lucy, aged nineteen, was also regarded by her family as the problem. She had a diagnosis of depression and anxiety and had returned home after apparently failing in her first year at university where she was studying psychology. She was tall and thin and had lost quite a bit of weight. She was also very intelligent and had got top grades in her A levels. Her tutors did not think she was failing because of a lack of ability.

Her GP had referred her as he thought she might need some individual psychotherapy.

After my first meeting with Lucy I discussed her with my team as was our usual practice. We were about to allocate her an individual therapist when something from my family therapy training prompted me to ask a question:

M: What if this is a family problem and Lucy's failure is alerting us to difficulties between them? So, it's not so much that there are problems at university for Lucy. Perhaps it's more about her leaving home that has disturbed something in the way the family normally related to each other. Lucy, then, is what family therapists call the 'identified patient'. Take one important card out of a house of cards and it all collapses.

A one degree, temperature change in an ocean is intimately linked to the destruction of a rain forest thousands of miles away.

We decided to see the whole family together.

M: Thank you Lucy for bringing your family here so that we can all understand what is going on.

This first statement is designed to start in the right frame. We wanted Lucy to feel appreciated and not continue to see herself as the problem or a burden and the family to begin wondering what is happening between them. We tried to convey that the whole family is the patient.

In systemic family therapy we notice that systems find their own balance ... called homeostasis. Had Lucy's departure to university upset the family equilibrium?

The family is also thanked for being willing to sit down together and be open to exploring what was going on. We are now like the doctor whose patient presents with a headache. Going beyond the symptom and being curious about the source of the problem, the doctor discovers the patient has a splinter in his foot causing him to limp. This has affected the muscles in his legs, back and neck causing a tension headache. Lucy's 'failure' is the symptom of a problem in the family system. As such, this can be welcomed as bringing the source of the problem to everyone's attention.

M: Lucy, thanks for alerting us to some issues that are occurring in your family. It's great that you've all come in today and have agreed to a series of meetings to help resolve them.

As these problems got highlighted by Lucy's moving away how about we represent that here? Lucy, would you sit as far away from your family as you can and for a moment or two just look back at them? And Mum and Dad and Dan, would you look at Lucy on the other side of the room for a few moments? Thank you.

Take your time to notice what you're feeling and thinking and then say anything that comes to mind if you want to.

After a minute or so:

Dan: It'd be more real if Lucy had her back to us!

M: Maybe say something like that to her?

Dan: You've turned your back on me and Mum and Dad!

(Lucy and her mum look tearful)

M: Can you say some more, Dan.

D: You're my best mate.

M: You look a mixture of sad and angry, Dan ... what it's like to have your best mate leave you?

D: It sucks! ... You know I don't have anyone else to talk to like we do. I can tell you anything. You understand me. Other people think I don't go out because I'm lazy, and am overweight because I'm greedy.

M: Lucy I can see you're upset. Can you say anything to Dan?

L: I feel completely stuck ... And it's not just Dan ... when I look from here ... it's like you all need me in different ways. I sort of like it and need you too but it also feels like a burden. How can I be free to live my own life?

M: How do Mum and Dad need you?

L: Mum and I have long chats having a secret fag in the kitchen. She tells me about her and Dad. I'm glad she can talk to me 'cos she not very happy ... but I feel a bit uncomfortable ...

M: and Dad?

L: We share a passion for jazz ... finding music online for each other and going out to gigs most weeks.

M: So Lucy, as you look back across the room at your family and let yourself feel these needs and connections ... take your time.

L: (Looking slowly at Dan and mum and dad in turn) I feel ... I ... I can't say ...

M: Look at me and tell me.

L: It's like ... like a huge magnet ... I can't escape it.

M: Go on.

L: I don't think they can manage without me ... wow that sounds a bit big-headed!

M: Try not to judge what you're feeling ... let it flow ...

L: I know they want me to succeed and live my own life but they all need me so much.

M: Sounds to me like you're in a bind. Damned if you do ... damned if you don't. If you leave, as you tried to, your family are going to suffer and if you stay you don't get to live your life. So really rather than failing, you've sacrificed your life for them.

L: But I wasn't coping ... I was anxious all the time.

M: Yes, but maybe anxious about your family and your loss of role ... you're already the family psychologist with a clear job to do with each of them ... unpaid though!

L: So how do I get out of the bind?

M: You don't, that's the point ... no win means no win!

L: Oh.

M: But something interesting happens when we truly accept this position and accept our helplessness.

L: I don't understand.

M: Don't worry too much about understanding but have a sense of letting go of struggle ... letting go of the role. Stop trying to fix things and see what emerges as you let go.

L: Okay, I'll try.

M: That's Lucy's homework for the next couple of weeks. I have some for you three too.

Dan ... your task is to find something you'd like to do with your dad that you would both enjoy.

Mum and Dad's homework is to go on a date ... I'll leave the details up to you ... Dad ... think of it as that old-fashioned word 'courting'.

(Next session – two weeks later)

M: Okay, how are things going?

Mum: Not great ... we did go out for a meal but didn't have

anything to say to each other!

Dan: Dad and I went to a film but he got a work call as we came out of the cinema, spoke for about half an hour, so I just came home.

M: Lucy?

L: I think I'd normally feel sorry for them at this point ... but I just feel ... well ... angry ...

M: Can you tell them?

L: That sounds pathetic! You can all do better than that!

(To therapist) I feel a strong pull to step in and fix it.

M: Stay with that ... let yourself accept the feeling however intense.

L: (Starts to cry and says through the tears) I just feel so helpless ... they're so unhappy ...

M: In the first meeting Dan said it felt like you turned your back on the family. Would you please go over to the corner again but this time with your back to the family?

L: Okay.

(Lucy sits in this position for a long time and then starts to cry, which becomes a sobbing ... she eventually turns round and although does not say anything, she looks quite different ... lighter and unburdened)

M: Okay, that's all for today everyone – thank you – see you in a couple of weeks.

A week later I received a brief letter.

Dear Martin,

Thank you so much for meeting with me and my family. Things have been tough for us all since the last meeting and I don't think we'll come again. But I feel like something has lifted and I've decided to go back to uni next month.

Best wishes

Lucy

Dear Lucy,

Thank you for letting me know. Well done to you and your family for having the courage to face this painful time and for exposing some issues that have been hidden by your role as caretaker.

I wish you all the best at university and for the future, and also hope that your brother and parents can come through this difficult transition and find the help and support that they need from each other and maybe from psychological services.

Best wishes

Martin

I did not hear any more about Lucy or her Dad but our team did hear that Dan took an overdose of paracetamol later that year and spent a few days in hospital recovering, and Lucy's mum had some counselling for depression in primary care not long after Lucy left home.

* * *

The astronomer Fred Hoyle once said that the chances of life existing on Planet Earth is the equivalent of placing twenty-seven fruit machines next to each other, pulling all the handles and them all coming up cherries. Everything has to be just right. The earth needs to be a certain distance from the sun, the moon's stabilising influence on the earth, the earth needs to have a molten core, vast amounts of water, even Jupiter is involved hoovering up the odd comet for us … etc., etc.

Everything in Nature is in balance … everything in us is in balance. A tiny granule out of place in the inner ear and we lose our balance and will fall.

Fragments trying to understand that which has no fragmentation is a great comedy.

Wu Sin

Lucy leaving for university upset the delicate eco system of her family. She had been playing a key role in maintaining that balance. Incidentally, this role provided her with an inner security as she set off into the unknown world of adulthood. Her family needed her and she needed to be needed. There was a co-dependency which in itself is not a problem and provides a balance. The problem is in the area of growth and change. Look closely at Nature and everything is growing, decaying and changing at vastly different speeds.

The change in Lucy and her family threatens the structure like a chick emerging from its shell. This is, of course, also perfect but, to the human mind the loss of structure appears as a problem to be fixed.

The mind does not generally acknowledge our natural intelligence. We set quite a lot of store in IQ but much less in Nature's fundamental capacity for survival and restoration. In one of David Attenborough's programmes, he was in the African savanna where it had not rained for five years. He dug up a clump of earth, broke it open to reveal a fish. This fish had lowered its metabolism to almost zero and was waiting for the rains to come ... at which point he will swim off into the newly formed lake.

Lucy's 'problem' and the way it brought the family for help was also perfect. The individual members were out of balance, lost and unfulfilled. Her struggle to leave has brought the family members' problems to light. The wallpaper has been stripped off and the cracks are clearly visible.

Things may need to get 'worse' for a while. Their loneliness and fears may need to be more deeply felt. Hopefully, though, not in the way that any of this might be viewed as failure but as their intuitive attempts to restore balance.

Lucy will have learnt a really important lesson as she starts out on her training. Namely that when we attend to our own need to be needed, we no longer need to be an expert or a family therapist, to be seen as wise, helpful, important etc. We then simply offer a mirror to the other person and remind them of their own resources.

At the end of 'The Wizard of Oz' the wizard is exposed by Dorothy's dog as just a little bald man with a microphone. He tells them they do not need any magic from him, and in order to have found him they already have what they are seeking ... the courage, the intelligence, the heart and the inner security, a 'home'.

Alongside this, Lucy may also learn to accept her personal powerlessness and to trust a power far greater than the individual ... the power of Nature.

The major problems in the world are the result of the difference between how nature works and the way people think.
Gregory Bateson

Chapter 13

Group Therapy: No Man Is an Island

'The group is the patient' my supervisor barked.

'Don't focus on the individuals and their thoughts and feelings ... they are simply expressing something for the whole group.'

Although, at the time, I was sceptical about this approach there was something about it that felt right. The group was more than a collection of individuals. As so often happens, a conversation in the next group I was leading mirrored the dialogue in my own head.

Group member 1: I don't think as a group we are very welcoming of new members.

GM2: Will you stop saying 'we'. Say 'I' ... Speak for yourself!

GM3: Yes and I don't think that's true anyway. I'm glad about the two new people that have started recently.

GM1: But I can see we have a certain pattern with new members.

GM2: Don't project your stuff on me! – You don't know what I'm thinking and feeling. Own it! Say 'I'.

Therapist (Martin): Maybe you are talking about two aspects of being in a group. Yes, there are individual members and yes, there is a group culture – something that we share.'

GM2: Don't you start!

M: There seems to be a strong resistance to the idea of 'we' ... maybe a 'fear' ... of losing something ... identity perhaps?

GM1: That's interesting 'cos what I see is that 'we' make it hard for new members to be themselves ... they have to fit in ... go through a sort of initiation.

GM2: That's crap!

GM3: Yes, we do welcome new members.

M: How about we hear from them?

GM5: Well, mostly I have felt welcome but there is something – I can't put my finger on it.

GM6: I can't see it. I have felt very accepted by the others.

GM5 to GM1: Can you describe what you see happening?

GM1: Well … us established members, me included, often put you two in the role of 'patient' with us in the role of therapists. You then are under pressure to conform … to fit in with the way we do things.

So, it looks like we're welcoming you, and in some ways we are … but there are conditions.

And this creates a hierarchy … we're calling you 'new' members … at worst, it's like boarding school where the sixth formers initiate the new boys into the ways of the school.

GM2: (A little less forcefully than before) You're still saying us.

M: In some ways 'new' members joining means that there is a completely new group … new members automatically changing the culture with what they bring.

(Next group a week later)

After a few moments' silence at the start of the group.

GM3: Did anyone hear the interview on the radio this morning? An MP is putting forward a bill to require all immigrants to learn English.

GM6: That's shocking!

(Mumbles of agreement in the group)

M: I wonder if, in a way, the group is coming back to the theme that was here last week?

After a long silence.

GM4: I thought a lot about last week's group. I do genuinely feel welcoming of new members but it's not the whole picture … and talking of pictures, my Mum sent me an old photo this week. In it I'm about seven and holding my newly born younger brother. I'm smiling but if you look closely it's not really a smile, more of a grimace ... it says 'if there was no one looking I'd throw this little pink thing out of the window ... seven years of feeling special and he comes along!'

I don't like to think of that going on in the group or being seen in that way.

GM2: (Tearful) You've just reminded me that there is a story in our family of my sister being found with her hands round my throat as I lay in my cot. I think in a way she has always hated me. I could never be her equal. Nowadays it's much more subtle ... but as a kid it was brutal.

Yeah, like you I don't like to think that I would ever be in her role to others!

GM3: I came home from the shops yesterday. My two-year-old reached into my shopping bag and pulled out some baby clothes for her sister who is due to be born next month. I said, 'No that's not for you it's for the baby.' She looked pissed off, turned around with her baby doll under her arm and threw it across the kitchen floor shouting: 'no baby, no way baby!'

M: Ha, Ha ... kids are wonderfully free of the self-judgements and inhibitions! I wonder if the group is seeking that kind of freedom?

GM3: But isn't that anarchy if we're just free to do what we like.

GM1: You're not free to shout fire in a crowded cinema.

M: What does that mean here in this group.

GM2: Maybe it means that we ... oh shit, I said we! ... That we can have the freedom to feel what we feel but need to consider the other person and their feelings as well.

GM6: As a 'new' member I'd rather people were honest about their feelings of hostility rather than pretending and these feelings coming out in other ways.

GM7: Yeah, it also feels less personal. It's not me people are resisting but anyone joining ... any disturbance to the status quo.

GM1: Actually I have felt resistant to 'new' people but I

don't want others to see that side of me ... I want to be seen as welcoming.

I think I get overly helpful to the new people to hide my hostility.

GM7: Yeah, but funnily enough, when you do that I feel patronised and in an odd way kept on the outside of you longer-standing members.

GM6: I feel like I'm always trying to prove something ... prove that I can make a contribution.

GM2: Is that why you go on and on about your work?

GM6: (Tearful) I guess so ... It's my whole identity!

M: Sounds like the group is getting to face some of the primitive feelings that get stirred up when people get together like this ... like in our families too?

GM2: Yes ... it feels a bit shameful but sort of freeing to talk about it here.

M: Well, you're being honest with yourselves and each other and accepting of some natural but difficult feelings. When these feelings are faced and fully accepted in the way you're starting to do, they don't need to be acted on and the tension around who's in and who's out can dissolve.

Without resistance and conditions, we all belong to the group just as we are ... there is nothing to prove, no tests to pass and new people no longer pose a threat to the status quo.

* * *

The task we must set for ourselves is not to feel secure but to be able to tolerate insecurity.
Erich Fromm

Fromm was writing at the time of the rise of Fascism in Europe. The therapy group is like a microcosm of bigger groups and the wider culture. If new people joining a group or immigrants entering a country are not a threat, then their presence enriches through difference and variety. If we can tolerate the insecurity that difference and change bring there is openness, harmony and creativity.

Only one thing is certain – Impermanence!
Buddha

Having a role, even that of Victim, provides some security for us in a group. We think we know who we are and how we will respond. Without this there is nothing to cling on to and the next thing that happens or is said is unpredictable, leaving us vulnerable. We generally fear the unknown even though it means freedom and offers a genuine intimacy as relating is now no longer role to role.

Also, a role is only a partial expression of who we are – a fragment. A group therapist who sees the group as the patient is not overly interested in individual concerns as these are merely fragments of the whole picture. These concerns are not viewed as problems but unconscious, fundamentally creative, attempts by the group to find balance and union.

The therapist trusts that Nature is re-establishing balance in the way it spontaneously does and that behind the superficial differences is an inherent belonging to the human family.

Differences in the group are acknowledged by the facilitator but, at the same time, used to remind members of their shared roots and true nature. In this process separation and isolation come to be seen as illusions of the mind, and groups and communities can begin to appreciate the common thread that connects us all.

Chapter 14

Staff Group Facilitation: A Dream for the Team

There never seemed to be enough chairs for the monthly staff group that I facilitated. Team members would scurry off to find extra chairs from other rooms in the building, bring their prize back and squeeze it into the tiny room that the ten or so of us met in. Like the majority of NHS rooms that I have sat in over the years there were no pictures and no plants. Often justified these days by health and safety policies. 'A patient might break off a twig of the plant and stab you or themselves with it!'

Despite the environment, I love team facilitation meetings for many reasons. Mostly because they are a rare chance for a team to come together and reflect on their work and how they related to each other. Also it often felt like being a detective ... sitting with them trying to find the source of their difficulties. Going beyond the every-day fire fighting and wondering about the cause of the fire.

What was less easy to sit with in these meetings was a general feeling of being demoralised and of hopelessness.

One thing I noticed that was common in staff groups were the team issues, often mirroring the patient group that they were working with. A group who worked with the elderly struggled with feelings of passivity and of not being heard or valued. A team that worked with adolescents often brought issues of power and identity ... and battles with authority.

The team I was with on this occasion were involved with helping with the rehabilitation of long-term mental health patients and often felt powerless and ignored. The staff team were physically present but were like a group of lost souls not sure of why there were there in the work anymore. It was painful to sit amongst highly skilled and compassionate colleagues who felt so demotivated. Naturally, the conversation often turned to thinking about some action or strategy that could make things better for them. These always felt like papering over the cracks but perhaps better than sitting with the pain and the loss of passion for the work. At times I also welcomed these attempts at solutions ... at least we were doing something! At least the team felt joined in a common task and cracks that are papered over cannot be seen anymore.

At one meeting one of the older women members of the team said:

'I had a dream last night. I was in an NHS building which was more like a warehouse. There were hundreds of staff sitting at their computers manically typing away. When I looked up, the ceiling was an exact replica of the Sistine Chapel ... God and man reaching out touching finger to finger. I shouted: "Look up!" But no one did. Everyone carried on typing.'

It was the first time anyone had brought a dream to these meetings and in the lengthy silence that followed it seemed as though team members were getting their heads around this means of communication and the images in the dream.

At the end of the silence I offered a possible interpretation of the dream:

'I wonder if the dream might remind us of something that's being ignored, forgotten. Something fundamental. Like the connection between each other and between whatever we think of as God, Love or Nature?'

There was another silence.

After a while a team member said:

'It reminds me that I've forgotten why I came into this work in the first place. I didn't do it to be sitting at a computer, spending hours on administration. What drew me was being able to make a difference in people's lives.'

Another team member looked a little tearful and said:

'Yes, I came into the work to help people, reach out to them in a way that enables them to live more fully again.'

M: Notice that in the dream it's not that something is missing, it's just that everyone's attention is drawn to the screen and not the ceiling. You've not lost the reasons you came into the work … simply forgotten them. The dream is a powerful reminder.

* * *

In the next hour every member of the team spoke about why they had become a nurse or a doctor or a psychologist. The quality of the meeting was different from usual. As a colleague of mine once said, it changed from a sense of grievance to grief. The team were no longer talking in a depressed way, for example flat and expressionless but feeling the deep sadness of what had been forgotten. This sort of grieving highlights what matters most to us and often brings us back to what is important in life.

Blessed are the mourners.
Jesus Christ (Matthew 5:4)

It is easy for any organisation to forget the patient or the customer and get distracted by the needs of the organisation. Senior managers in a large organisation like the NHS are a long way from the coal face and need to establish healthy finances, safe practices and good record keeping. This team, like others, felt overwhelmed by the organisational needs that came from above and felt demoralised and powerless. They were left with a sense of grievance but felt they had no voice.

The dream is brought by an individual member of the team but is a gift to the whole team. It is often said in sporting circles that there is no 'I' in team. The individual is just the instrument through which the dream comes. The dream also seemed to bring people together. They were united in their loss and united in their passion for the work, which, through the images in the dream could now be shared.

The team had been restructured the year before. This was the result of a national initiative and came with certain practices and policies. This brought massive changes in personnel. Interestingly, the team was disbanded a couple of years later and the staff group dispersed. Having worked in social services and the NHS for over forty years, I have seen this type of re-organisation many times. The restructuring usually comes with high hopes that 'the answer' had been found.

The staff were often faced with significant changes to their working practices, work environment and team personnel. For them, it often seemed like the changes carried a hidden message that they were not doing a good enough job the way things were and needed to change.

What the dream could also be reminding us of is what never changes. The images goes back to the beginning of time to when God gives life to Adam. But Adam, in gaining knowledge, starts to see himself as separate and leaves the Garden of Eden.

I have never met anyone who came into NHS work for the money. Many of us joined because of our own sense of isolation. Our own wounds. But through this comes the desire to help others who are isolated, the potential for a deep connection to our patients and a shared loss of connection to our true nature ... to love and union.

Because of our own separation we see everything through this lens – a collection of individuals seeing our individual patients. What if we were to step back and see the bigger picture? We might see a collective malaise.

In a chapter called 'Fragmentation and Wholeness' David Bohm, a theoretical physicist, describes this problem:

It is especially important to consider this question today, for fragmentation is now very widespread, not only throughout society, but also in each individual: and this is leading to a kind of confusion of the mind, which creates an endless series of problems and interferes with our clarity of perception so seriously as to prevent us from being able to solve most of them.

Or ... two and a half thousand years before Bohm:

As long as we are mesmerised by the tree, the root cannot be understood.
Wu Hsin

Separateness is a problem of perception. In reality we are not separate. Every time we breathe in and out we confirm this. We depend on Nature, each other and the world around us for life. The question is 'How do we remind ourselves?'

Chapter 15

Social Dreaming: Revealing the Collective Unconscious

Imagine sitting in a large group of people and feeling free to say whatever you felt like and as much or as little as you wanted.

I can still vividly remember my first social dreaming group which was nearly twenty years ago. There were at least forty of us in the room and the person leading the group only gave a few simple instructions. We were to sit in a random pattern in the room. We would start with someone volunteering a dream, which they told in the first person and in the present. We were invited to have associations to the dream and to the chain of associations that followed. We were told not to offer opinions or interpretations. You were allowed to speak as much or as little as you liked.

There was something about what happened in that group that fascinated me. I had been a member of all sorts of groups over the years but this was unlike any other. I started to do some research and found a colleague, Adena, who shared my love for social dreaming. We have since hosted several at conferences and for organisations.

The practice was developed in 1982 by Gordon Lawrence who was a group analyst. Since then this process has been used in many different settings including in post-Apartheid South Africa where it apparently enabled people to go past their differences and find a commonality that transcended the ethnic and political differences that were dividing them.

Our dreams offer infinite insight into the world we live when shared ... The infinite is the unknown, and the dream introduces us to this: it questions what we have assumed, and

accepted to be social knowledge.
Gordon Lawrence

The night before I was about to start writing this chapter, I had a dream:

I am with a large group of people who are all associated with a very rich and powerful man. He chooses me as a close ally and wants me to look after his dog which has been reconstructed by surgery to his requirements.

The immediate association I have to this dream is to a character in a TV drama called Goliath in which William Hurt plays a brilliant lawyer who lives in the dark in a penthouse above the firm in which he is a partner. His face is disfigured from being burnt in Vietnam. He is powerful but manipulative, increasingly isolated and ultimately destroyed by his own arrogance.

In keeping with the theme of this chapter, I am not going to attempt to interpret this dream or think about it in any way that is analytical. But leave it in the background to see what emerges by way of associations. The reader might like to have associations of their own to the dream images.

Associating is unlike other types of logical thinking. We are not asking ourselves 'what does that remind me of?' We simply notice what arises spontaneously and intuitively.

We have found that participants would often comment that the process was more like a meditation and day dreaming where the functional mind can take a back seat. Social dreaming groups are unlike other social groups where there can be a pressure to speak or to say something 'valuable', clever or witty. In those groups we are often comparing ourselves to others. Also, in social groups and organisations there are hierarchies in which some people's comments and opinions are given more weight and others less.

In keeping with this, in social dreaming the group 'leaders' are called 'hosts'. As hosts, we simply set the context and the guidelines and keep the time and space boundaries. We are not experts, have no agenda or desired outcomes.

We trust that the unconscious will be the 'leader' for us all, that the dream or dreams and associations will bring what is needed to consciousness. We are not interested in who says what, just that images arise.

We have also noticed that, in the second half of the process, when the group meets after a break to discuss what they experienced in the first part the 'dreaming' aspects of the dreaming part remain. The discussion usually feels free from competitiveness and agitation. The tranquil pace and the quality of listening spills over into the discussion group. There is an interest in *the* unconscious rather than *my* unconscious … in *we* rather than *me*.

When Adena and I realised we were going to attend the same conference in Germany we offered to host a social dreaming group.

Social dreaming group: Frankfurt – 2012

The room we had been given was drab, dirty and shabby. Only one person turned up at the start time, the other ten (we were expecting a lot more) came in one by one.

First session – fifty minutes:

'Does anyone have a dream that they'd like to bring?'

One of the men in the group raised his hand.

'Yes, I had a dream last night.'

'Thank you.'

'I am in a lift which gets stuck halfway to its journey to the top floor. I manage to get out and see a young blonde man with a gun who then shoots a woman. I run away and come to a square where a group of young men are kicking another young man to death. I run to what seems to be a safe house nearby.'

(Five minutes silence)

'It reminds me of visiting a holocaust memorial yesterday and thinking about my Jewish family and what happened to them.'

'At the memorial I was struck by so many victims without names.'

'I'm remembering stories that my grandparents told me.'

'I thought of my German uncle who died on the Russian front aged 21 ... his body was never found.'

(Twenty minutes silence)

'I'm reminded of a time when I was abused and my only solace was to see birds outside my window.'

'I was struck by the absence of birds when we went to Auschwitz.'

(Fifteen minutes silence)

Group hosts: Okay, it's time for that part of the group to end. We'll take a break now and come back to discuss our experiences.

In this break Adena and I were in a sort of state of shock. We had led several social dreaming groups before. In all of these the associations had flowed easily. With her Jewish background and my German history and holding this group in Frankfurt, we had expected these themes to emerge but were quite unprepared for the intensity of the group and of the silences. The air was so heavy. What was so unspeakable? Almost everything!

In these breaks we were normally excited about the process and anticipating the discussion to follow. This time we were anxious and almost reluctant about returning to the group for the second part. We both shared that we had gone in and out of so many feelings particularly fear and anger, but mostly a strange absence of feeling ... a deadness, emptiness, desolation and powerless.

When we did return, we set the scene for the second half:

'The next part of the group is a space in which we can discuss our experiences of the group before the break. As in the first part, feel to say as much or as little as you like.'

(Two minutes silence)

'I couldn't speak ... just could not say a word. Also I had to look out of the window ... It was just too painful to look into the room ... I'm sorry.'

'I'm glad you said that because I'd read your looking out of the window as indifference.'

'No, no ...' (looks tearful).

'I also couldn't speak ... I think because I'm English ... I sort of felt I did not have the right to say anything ... it's not logical but like it was not to do with me.'

'I couldn't speak because I'm German and felt a heavy burden of responsibility.'

'I notice that in the dream the lift got stuck ... and then it was like we were all stuck ... stuck in the past ... stuck with guilt and shame ... stuck in rage and injustice.'

'I felt those feelings too but also completely powerless.'

'It occurs to me that people's silence played a part in these atrocities continuing ... but now I don't feel so judging of that ... it's so powerful, so impossible ... what can you say?'

'You're saying something now ...'

'Yes, I feel released by talking about this and by hearing how we were all stuck. I don't have to take it personally ... and feel so ashamed.'

'I felt so alone when I was looking out of the window ... but it was like I literally could not do anything else!'

'I guess we're all capable of being the victim, the perpetrator or the bystander?'

(Several minutes' silence in which many of the group look tearful – the quality of this silence seemed less stuck, more reflective and more connected)

'I've been thinking about why I can't let myself enjoy Frankfurt ... I think it's because it would somehow feel like being disloyal to my Jewish grandparents.'

'As a young German, I really want you to enjoy my city, my country. I want you to let go of the past otherwise we're all stuck!'

The second part of the group had felt very different. Nothing had been solved but something powerful and divisive had dissolved. People seemed to have come together in a shared grief. We had also shared a powerlessness and a shame allowing us all to move through the stuckness mentioned in the original dream and the last comment.

* * *

We are the night ocean filled
With glints of light. We are the space
between the fish and the moon
while we sit here together.
Rumi

Each time we have hosted or been participants in social dreaming groups the same thing has happened. When human beings are restricted in terms of the 'I' thought ... not 'allowed' to pass personal judgement or opinion, what connects us rather than what divides us comes into awareness. Within a few minutes of people sitting together in this way we start to talk about what is shared. We start to bring issues of life and death, of fear and shame, of love and harmony, confinement and freedom. The foreground issues of life fall away and the background is revealed. We could even say the illusion of separateness dissolves and the reality of interconnectedness comes into view.

It is that 'my' consciousness is not just my consciousness meaning the consciousness produced by **my** brain, any more than a programme produced over the air, would be a programme produced by my TV set.
Irvin Laslo

The group in Frankfurt reminds us of the most extreme examples of man's inhumanity to man. Of what happens when fear, shame and ignorance become prejudice, when other human beings become objects to be disposed of. When we cannot remember without blame and prejudice ... all of us stuck in our histories, not able to connect to the human being that sits next to us.

Social dreaming is a process that can remind us of what is always present just beyond the narrow concerns of the individual ego. It simply offers a different lens ... a more global view for the so called individual mind.

When the wall between two dissolves,
That which sources both is revealed.
Wu Hsin

If I come back to the dream I had before writing this chapter, I can see it maybe pictures the worst excesses of the individual ego. That we are better than Nature and can manipulate it. That our power corrupts leaving us with a sense of being above others ... but ultimately leaves us separate and alone. Donald Cooperman, the character played by William Hurt, both literally and psychologically falls at the end of the series. Nature lasts ... ego does not! Like Shelley's 'Ozymandias' all that remains left in the desert is some rubble, the feet and the writing on the plinth that used to be a massive statue.

My name is Ozymandias, King of Kings;
Look on my Works, ye Mighty, and despair!
Nothing beside remains. Round the decay
Of that colossal Wreck, boundless and bare
The lone and level sands stretch far away.
Percy Bysshe Shelley

I remember before one social dreaming group I was looking at a map of London to get directions to the venue. I noticed that the Thames begins from way beyond the city, flows through the centre and out to the sea.

I thought of the social dreaming process as similar. We sit together and simply allow the thoughts and associations to come from beyond us without a need to generate or personally create anything. There is then just a flow through the body and mind (without too much interference) and out to the sea joining an ocean of consciousness.

This is a spontaneous flow without the need for interpretation or analysis and even without the need for expression.

My mother's home town of Königsberg is now part of Russia and called Kaliningrad. Most of the original town was destroyed by the allies in 1944, no Germans remained and it is now populated by Russians. All the names of the streets and areas are, of course, Russian. However, the river is still there, still called the Pregel regardless of what is happening beyond its banks.

The infinite flow of consciousness continues unaffected by the comings and goings of human beings and our ignorance.

But if we are willing to listen to our dreams then *the* unconscious rather than *my* unconscious will remind us of the interconnectedness that lies beyond our individual minds.

Chapter 16

The Mysterious Matching of Patients to Therapists: All Is One

Is there a universal force that brings people together? Where like attracts like ... where 'chance' meetings turn out to bring together people who seem to belong together.

A few years ago some colleagues and I ran a one-year psychotherapy training programme in the NHS. As part of the programme we needed to match patients to trainees hoping to find a good pairing. The course ran for eight years with twelve trainees each year, meaning a total of over a hundred pairings were needed.

Initially we spent several hours at the beginning of each course attempting to match the right therapist with each patient. We were trying to give the patient the best experience possible by finding them a therapist with whom they had something in common ... someone who could relate to their life challenges ... someone who could resonate with their emotional life and painful traumas.

We knew very little about the trainees so were basing this matching on age, gender, whether they were parents etc. We soon discovered that there was a more mysterious matching going on at the same time.

We noticed each year that, in spite of our attempts at matching, the right patient invariably ended up with the right therapist, as though some universal force was bringing them together ... like attracting like. Details emerged that we could not have known about. For example, we knew very little about the trainees' personal lives or histories.

Curious connections came to light that we hadn't anticipated: One patient had a powerful envy of her sister; the trainee's sister had envied her when they were children.

Another patient's mother was extremely critical and undermining – the trainee's mother used identical words to criticize her and their mothers had the same Christian name.

One of the trainees had bright red hair – the patient said during the therapy, 'I was so glad you have red hair as my father's relatives all have red hair … I love that side of the family.'

The main issue for one patient was that her husband was having an affair – the trainee therapist she had been allocated to, came to her supervisor concerned that he too was on the brink of having an affair.

These are just a few of the many examples that prompted us to stop trying to match patients to trainees and allow the magical process to happen naturally.

The trainees, for whom this was their first psychotherapy patient would often say to me: 'I'm sure my patient would be better off seeing someone more experienced like you.'

I would always say: 'You're the best person! I know it's hard to believe but, in my experience, it's not an accident that you came together at this time. Just tune in to the resonance between you and be open to the meaning in the apparent coincidence.'

In the therapy supervision groups, we would hear how the relationship between patient and trainee was unfolding and how the patient's life struggles often curiously mirrored those of the therapist they had been matched with. We also noticed that the patient would often echo insights that had already taken place in conversation between the therapist and me in supervision. It was as if the patient themselves had been present in the supervision group!

* * *

Matchings at work – an example

Gill (trainee therapist): My patient is getting more and more stressed at work. He's a social worker and takes on new cases even though he's burning out. If he says 'no' he feels guilty. So, then he gets sick and has to take time off.

She paused.

That pattern is so like me! But it means I don't know what to say to him ... if I did, I could say it to myself!

M: Jung once said that there was no change in the patient unless there was change in the analyst. If we stop viewing this as the well treating the sick, we might see both of you coming together to face something deep in your history. To understand what drives you to be in the role of helper. This way therapy is a mutual experience of learning and in the process the opportunity of freedom from the role.

G: I think I can see from my own therapy what is at the heart of this. It's not just that my patient and I have similar patterns at this point in our lives but we both have a history of abuse and neglect. Our experiences were very different in the detail but very similar in the stories that we created around what happened to us. I know I never felt noticed or good enough and my mum spent a lot of time in a psychiatric hospital. Looking after her was tough and never very effective but it was the only thing that gave me a sense of importance. Looking back, without this I felt like a nobody!

M: So the compulsion to help hides the fear of being a nobody and maybe of being powerless?

G: Yes ... I think it does (Gill's voice becomes quiet).

M: Do you feel a drive to help your patient?

G: Yes, it's very strong!

M: So in a way you and your patient are trying desperately to help others. Do you think you might subtly be agreeing 'Let's both hide our fears of being a nobody ... and of feeling powerless'?

G: Yes, I guess so ... he's probably feeling similar to me underneath.

M: So, paradoxically, you could help him most by not trying to help him.

G: Ergh?

M: He needs to know that he's fine just as he is. Not constantly trying to prove he is okay by being a saint and a martyr ... and of course you need to know the same! That your presence is enough!

Maybe, as you sit with him, notice the impulse to help, give advice or come up with solutions. Sit with the feelings that arise when it feels like you are doing nothing. Watch any fears surface.

G: (After the next therapy session) What you suggested last time wasn't an easy thing to do or not do. I notice I'm wanting to help the whole time ... to make it better for him. It's painful just sitting there feeling his pain. I could switch off from it which I did for a bit but that didn't seem right.

M: It's about the balance of love and wisdom. The love is the resonance with the other person and their pain. And wisdom is the capacity to step back and see the bigger picture. So, if our patient is in a pit of despair, we need to be in there with them so we can really know what it's like. This is the 'love' aspect. But if we're **only** in there with them then no one is seeing the bigger picture ... seeing beyond the pit. So, we also need to stand outside the pit which is the wisdom. Each on their own is limited.

The fact that you and your patient are so alike allows you to be in the pit with him and feel the intensity of his despair and hopelessness. But now we have two people in the pit with neither seeing anything more than its walls.

It's great you can identify with your patient but at the same time, as therapists, we need to dis-identify with their story and our story too!

G: What do you mean?

M: When we experience trauma there is a story that goes with it. Often some version of 'I'm not good enough'. With this goes a sense of hopelessness ... how will this ever change? Our personal pit of despair. We then find a way to counter this, cover it. In your case and your patient's and mine, incidentally, this was covered by a drive to be helpful ... to prove that we **are** good enough.

The combination of love and wisdom allows us to feel the full intensity of the story and at the same time loosen our identification with a belief that was never true.

Your freedom from your story and your drive to counter it is an invitation to your patient to experience that liberation too. There can then be a return to the stillness that was there before any story.

(Three months later)

G: I haven't said anything directly to my patient but he has been starting to talk about how driven he feels to help others. He's now noticing a compulsion to take on more work even when he has no space ... and even said last week ... 'I don't know who I am without this role in life' ... It's like he's been listening in on our conversations!

M: Well in a way he has. In general, we still apply a sort of Newtonian physics to psychiatry and psychotherapy ... like billiard balls hitting one against the other. Supervisor says something to trainee and trainee says something to patient etc. From Quantum physics we know that these changes take place across time and space ... it's called 'entanglement'.

In a way your patient **is** in the room with us changing as we change.

As awareness sheds a light on what each of us is caught with, this dissolves revealing a freedom that lies beyond any role.

* * *

Carl Jung, in an introduction to the ancient Chinese oracle the *I Ching*, wrote about coincidence. He compares two people walking along a beach when something washes up on the shore as they walk past. The first person, who is from the West, says: 'Oh something has washed up on the beach.' The other from the East says: 'Why has this thing washed up just as I walk past ... what is the meaning of this?'

> Synchronicity takes the coincidence of events in time and space as meaning something more than mere chance.
> C.G. Jung

Instead of seeing life as a collection of random events and chance meetings with others we could see these as manifestations of a unified whole. We would see everything as interconnected and nothing acting separately or individually. We could become curious about who or what arrives on our doorstep and see these as mirrors to our own wholeness ... parts of ourselves we have split off from returning to complete the picture.

With this perspective we are no longer struggling with the unwanted, uncomfortable aspects of life but instead welcoming home an old friend.

These events in life can act as guides to freedom by bringing us face to face with the aspects of our story that still trap us. It is as though we are walking along and a branch catches our clothing. We stop and face what it is that catches us. The facing and embracing of what we are repeatedly caught with ends the struggle and leads to a lasting freedom.

> Let us hope for the advent of a psychiatry which places the psychic crisis in a wider context, that of man in search of himself, a potentiality inherent in all of life's expressions. Psychiatry will then be able to fully inhabit its function, that of an awakener of consciousness and an artisan of peace.
> Dr Jean-Marc Mantel

Chapter 17

Mindfulness FAQs – The Gift of Disillusionment

Be patient toward all that is unsolved in your heart and try to love the questions themselves.

Rainer Maria Rilke, *Letters to a Young Poet*

When I was teaching mindfulness and meditation to NHS colleagues over thirty years ago it often felt as if I was suggesting witchcraft might help our patients!

Nowadays mindfulness is fully accepted as a treatment for depression, anxiety, pain management and other disorders. The practice is now being taught in lots of different settings including the army, schools, MPs and the corporate world.

Popularising this ancient philosophy and practice has been a great gift – especially for meditators like me working in the NHS. Now that mindfulness is included within the accepted NHS guidelines as a form of treatment we can hold mindfulness groups for patients and staff. One drawback of mindfulness being used as a treatment is that we might forget its origins: I heard a story of a senior psychologist in London who said that he thought the Dalai Lama should come to their department as he might learn something about how they were practising mindfulness!

The 'use' of mindfulness as a treatment puts it in the same bracket as other treatments within a medical model suggesting that something is wrong that needs fixing. Treatment implies a form of doing that takes us from one state to another so that we feel better. But the essence of mindfulness embodies the opposite, reminding us that there is nothing wrong and nothing to be fixed.

This perspective radically changes the common practice of conventional therapy as this contemporary Buddhist writer highlights.

But mindfulness meditation in its 'ultimate' application—as a Buddhist practice aimed toward realization of nibbana (non-attachment)—is not concerned with shaping a functional ego. It is, rather, a way to disidentify with both health and illness, happiness and sorrow, pleasure and pain.
C.W. Huntington Jr.

Is mindfulness being misused? Professor Mark Williams, whose research has played such a major part in the acceptance of mindfulness in the Health Service, was asked, in a radio interview, if he was concerned about potential misuses of this ancient practice to which he replied: 'No, mindfulness practice is inherently subversive.'

My understanding of what Williams means is that the simple practice of pure awareness undermines the common patterns of thought. For example, in the corporate world where mindfulness might be employed to increase productivity, sitting in stillness often highlights the contrast between a mind under pressure and a fundamental silent presence.

Being present with our fundamental stillness can lead to a profound disillusionment with our way of life … all the striving, manic busi-ness, searches for money or power, feelings of loneliness and inadequacy can be seen for what they are … creations of the human mind.

Ironically, the true source of the teaching and practice of mindfulness does not attempt to add or fix anything. It invites us to strip away illusion and reminds us of our true nature.

The wave forgets the truth that it is ocean, thinking itself to be the grand shape, which it has temporarily taken.

For a while, it takes on the rupa (form) of wave.
Finally, it remembers its true rupa (form) of ocean.
The two coexist, though one is true, and the
other, though beautiful, is only relatively true.
So too, we humans forget our true nature,
but, through yoga (union), can remember.
From the *Yoga Sutras of Patanjali*

* * *

Mindfulness has two integral aspects: the teaching or understanding and the practice. The 'subverting', to use Williams' word, of the mind's usual patterns is at the heart of mindfulness meditation. We can realise that we are not our thoughts and start to question who or what we truly are. This clarification often in groups or on retreats allows the whole group to question the creations of the mind:

Q: Is it possible to control my mind?

A: No, you won't control the mind. Buddhists call it 'monkey mind' jumping from tree to tree ... a whole chain of associations. But it's not a problem that we have thoughts, only that we get absorbed by them and identify with them.

Q: I don't think I can meditate because as soon as I sit down I have lots of random thoughts like what I'm going to buy for dinner tonight.

Q (Another member of the group): Yes, my mind is filled with thoughts ... some of them really negative. I try to push them away or distract myself but it only works for a few seconds. So, what should I do?

A: Simply observe them. Any attempt to manage them gives energy to the very things we want to be rid of.

Be like the snow globes you see at Christmas time. The thoughts are the flakes. The more you shake, the more you disturb them. Just set it down and its stillness and gravity does the rest. You're left with clarity.

Q: But some are so negative. I feel overwhelmed by them.

A: That's a really good example. We feel overwhelmed because of the identification. See them all as just thoughts. What does Hamlet say? 'There is nothing either good or bad, but thinking makes it so.'

Q: So what about trying to have positive thoughts?

A: There's no need – they're all just thoughts. Not who you really are.

Q: Some of them are horrible ... violent ... hateful.

A: When the horror movie ends there's no blood left on the screen. If a pneumatic drill starts up during your silent meditation there's no damage done to the silence. We're so often caught in the foreground of our awareness forgetting the background silence and the stillness.

Q: But I feel damaged by the traumas of my past. So, it's not easy to just ignore them or forget them.

A: I'm not suggesting you do that. Simply stop identifying with them as you. These things happened to you but you don't need to let them define you.

A: (From another member of the retreat) I suffered abuse and extreme neglect when I was young. I've been deeply affected by this but have realised there is a part of my being that is not damaged in any way!

Q: Thank you that's really helpful ... So Martin, is it as simple as that ... just notice?

A: Yes, be present and notice. In a way this is more simple than we could ever imagine. There's a story of two monks who left their monastery for a trip and on their return said to their teacher: 'Master the teacher at the nearby monastery can walk on water ... what can you do?'

'Well ... when I'm eating, I'm eating, and when I'm sleeping, I'm sleeping.'

He's reminding them that if we are truly in this moment,

there is no past or future, no story, no success or failure ... just being and openness.

Also, when we notice thoughts and feelings it brings into view the objects of awareness and awareness itself. Foreground observed from the background. The agitated mind and body observed from stillness. We couldn't know agitation and stress unless we were fundamentally still and peaceful. When we stand still on the railway station and a train passes at ninety miles per hour we know it's travelling very fast because of our stillness. If we did not know freedom, we could not experience the prison walls as confining us.

Q: How do I find stillness?

A: You can't find it. You are it! Any step taken is a step away from what you are.

Q: Then what do I do?

A: There's nothing to do!

Q: Ergh?

A: It's a paradox. Like the action of no action. There's a Sufi saying: 'Those who seek the Lord will never find him but those who don't seek the Lord will also never find him.'

Q: That doesn't make any sense! And I don't find it very helpful!

A: Our minds need to know – is it this or that, black or white? The paradox stops the mind in its usual attempts to know and allows another deeper knowing. The mind is frustrated and confused in the process ... so just allow this and maybe the stillness will find you.

Q: When I look around at the group I think 'they look a lot more relaxed than me'. Should I practise more or for longer?

A: There's a story of a woman who approached a meditation teacher and said 'How long will it take me to be enlightened?' The teacher says playfully 'Around ten years.' The woman asks 'Well, what if I try harder and do twice what everyone else does?' The teacher replies: 'Well then it would take you twenty years.'

This is not about effort or skills or technique. Only about remembering who or what you are!

In Zen there is the image of the 'beginner's mind', simple and uncluttered which even the most experienced meditator aspires to.

Q: Then why bother to practise at all?

A: Because those who don't seek the Lord will never find him. We often need to start with some form of practice and then over time let it go. The Buddha once said that if you have a thorn in your leg, use another thorn to get it out ... then throw them both away. We need the practice at the beginning as it gets us started but is not necessary after a while ... it's really the practice of no practice.

You can't practise being who you are. But you can know what you're not and when this falls away then be who you are!

Q: How does it fall away?

A: It falls away naturally in your awareness and with acceptance. Our true nature is revealed.

As far as we can tell the rest of Nature is not concerned about how to be or what to do. The bird is not concerned about how well it is singing. The dog is not worried about what his mother would think of his cat-chasing.

The human mind is a gift and a curse. We are capable of great achievements and cursed by the knowledge of 'I'. As in the story of Adam and Eve as soon as we know 'I' there is separation and shame. We feel separate ... disconnected.

Q: You've mentioned God and Buddha ... is this about religion?

A: No, religion is usually about prescriptions. We are talking here about perception not prescription. A local hospital chaplain gave a talk on this theme a few years ago and said: 'Religion is for people who are afraid of Hell ... spirituality is for people who've been there!'

Rather than living by prescription, study your misperceptions to know what is real. Go beyond the prescriptions to the source of the teachings whether it be Buddha, Christ, Krishna or Mohammed.

For example, here is a part of the Lord's prayer translated by Douglas Klotz from the original Aramaic:

Source of Sound: in the roar and the whisper,

In the breeze and the whirlwind, we hear your Name.

Radiant One: You shine within us,

Outside us – even darkness shines – when we remember.

Sounds a bit different from the version that we're used to doesn't it? Maybe because that version has gone through four different translations before it got to us? We can hear and see something else in the original.

Q: There are a lot of things about my life and my thoughts I don't want to see.

A: In Rumi's poem 'The Guest House' he encourages us to welcome every guest, even the ones who strip us of all our possessions as they may be 'clearing' us for some new experience.

Q: I've just lost my husband … am I supposed to welcome that?

A: Rumi wasn't saying that we should like what happens or feel no pain. His friend and mentor Shams of Tabriz was murdered. It's the opposite. Feel the pain deeply so that you can know the depth of love and loss in a way that opens you to what life brings next.

Also, what is knocking is already there so you may as well welcome it rather than resist … and even more importantly what is knocking is not separate from you … it's a part of you calling for attention.

Perhaps everything that frightens us is, in its deepest essence, something helpless that wants our love.

Rilke

Q: Acceptance of everything that comes our way feels like giving up.

A: We are not talking about passive resignation, but an opening of the arms and heart in an embrace. A deep trust in what comes as clearing us as Rumi says for 'some new delight'.

Q: I'm a musician and I sometimes feel like the music is playing me ... is that similar to what we're talking about here?

A: Yes, very. We can notice our breathing, for example. Are we doing breathing? Are we thinking I must breathe in and out? Or is it more like we are being breathed?

We are bamboo flutes through which the music (life) flows. Clear the flute and life flows easily ... the music plays with a clarity.

Q: I like to feel more in control than that.

A: Sorry to say that control is an illusion. As you say we might like to 'feel' in control but it's different in reality. My colleague Jean-Marc Mantel says this feeling is like the child in the back seat of a car with the little plastic steering wheel thinking he is in control. None of us know what will happen tomorrow despite having put all number of things in the personal planner.

Q: When we were just sitting here together you gave me permission to be still.

A: I didn't give you anything! It appears to the mind as if there is someone giving someone else permission to be still. But in reality, stillness is finding itself through us. Each question contains its own answer ... each permission is already present in the heart of the receiver. You were ready to hear it.

Q: Okay, but how does this work practically ... does this help me live my life differently?

A: Again don't try to live differently. Just let the source of your actions come from stillness ... the source of your words from silence. Be absent in a personal sense ... clear the flute. Then your words and actions are not influenced by your personal story but come free of the past.

Q: My personal story?

A: We each have a story formed early on in life. The psychologist Adler called this our 'guiding fiction'. We think of ourselves as inadequate, not good enough, unlovable, stupid etc. and these fictional thoughts can drive our whole life. See these for what they are and realise that you are not your story!

True intimacy is the absence of this story ... the absence of your role in your personal drama. Then there is no script, no set pattern of conversation ... the words come without agenda or expectation.

This, in turn, invites a freedom in the other person, or the family, group or team. The usual roles are now less fixed ... you being free of a role upsets the pattern and opens up new possibilities. What comes is in tune with the present moment – no longer informed by the past.

Q: My partner's relatives really let us down last week. We travelled miles to see them and they had changed the plan without letting us know. I tried to accept my anger but just felt furious and then bad for having those feelings.

A: This acceptance needs to be wholehearted and total. It's the heart rather than the head that's needs to be most involved and not only every aspect of what happened but also your feelings, your anger, needs to be fully accepted.

Remember we're not talking about liking what happens or what we feel but accepting and welcoming. Accept your non-acceptance!

Q: My mum's got dementia and I'm going to look after her for a while. We've always had a difficult relationship. One of my biggest worries is that I won't be able to do my regular practice and keep my sense of balance without being disturbed by her.

A: Maybe see her as your teacher, dressed in purple robes, giving you the perfect opportunity to feel your freedom whatever the circumstances, to know stillness in the midst of disturbance.

Ram Dass once said, 'If you think you're enlightened go and

spend a week with your parents.'

Q: Why don't you teach different themes each week or have an agenda for the course?

A: How would I know beforehand what the group will bring? … Like last week when you all spoke about your fathers and how they were absent either literally or emotionally. The group is like a flute too. What needs to flow through will come if we allow a space.

Q: Yeah, I hadn't realised how much I'd missed my dad until last week.

A: So, in the group, we all participate in opening up to what's needed and contribute to each other's openness too. Our collective stillness allows what is not still in us to surface and dissolve.

*   *   *

The practice of mindfulness encourages us to see the world as it really is … all one. In the meetings with individuals with couples, families and groups described in this book we can see that if we look deeply at our lives and relationships, we are all connected. Thich Nhat Hanh, perhaps the world's foremost mindfulness teacher calls this being mindful of our 'inter-being'.

With this lens we will inevitably start to question the usual view of a world of separate things and separate beings and see what is really there. Separateness is an illusion, reinforced by language and a sort of collective hypnosis. Our challenge is simply to wake up from this dream state and be true to who we really are.

To make Wu Hsin laugh,
One need merely talk
About one's feeling of
disconnection.

Wu Hsin sees the thirsty
fish.
Wu Hsin laughs and laughs.
The lost writings of Wu Hsin

References

Barks, C. (2006) *A year with Rumi, Daily readings*, Harper Collins, New York

Bateson, G. (2000) *Steps towards an Ecology of Mind*, The University of Chicago Press, Chicago, USA

Berne, E. (1972). *What do you say after you say hello?: The psychology of human destiny*, New York, NY: Grove Press

Bernie, J. (2010) *Ordinary Freedom*, Non-Duality press, Salisbury, UK

Bohm, D. (1980) Wholeness and the Implicate Order, Routledge and Kegan Paul, London and New York

Carse, D. (2005) *Perfect Brilliant Stillness*, Non-Duality press, Salisbury, UK

Cope, S. (1999) *Yoga and the Quest for the True Self*, Bantam, New York

Dalai Lama, Culter, H. (2009) *The Art of Happiness in a Troubled World*, Hodder and Stoughton, London, UK

Eliot, T.S. (1943) *The Four Quartets*, Faber and Faber, London

Finley, J. (2014) *Meister Eckhart's Living Wisdom: Indestructible Living Joy and the Path of Letting Go*, (Audio book) Sounds True, Boulder, Colorado, USA

Finley, J. (1978) *Merton's Palace of Nowhere*, Ave Maria Press, Notre Dame, Indiana, USA

Foulkes, S.F. (1983) *Introduction to group analytic therapy*, London: Karnac Books

Fromm, E (2001) *Fear of Freedom*, Routledge, London, UK

Huntington, C (2018) 'Are you Looking to Buddhism when you Should be Looking for Therapy?' *Tricycle Magazine*, Spring 2018 edition

Gangaji, (2011) *Hidden Treasure: Uncovering the Truth in your Life Story*, Penguin, New York

Hoyle, F. (1983) *Intelligent Universe: A new view of Creation and*

Evolution, Bundle Books, Michael Joseph Ltd, London.

Jung, C.G. (1985) *Synchronicity, An Acausal Connecting Principle*, Routledge, East Sussex, UK

Karpman, S (1968). 'Fairy tales and script drama analysis', *Transactional Analysis Bulletin*, 26 (7): 39–43

Klein, J. (2008) *The Book of Listening*, Non-Duality Press, Salisbury UK

Klotz, D. (1994) *Prayers of the Cosmos*, Thorsons, London

Laslo, E. (2017) *The Intelligence of the Cosmos*, Inner Traditions, Rochester, Vermont, USA

Lawrence, W. Gordon (ed.) (2007), *Infinite Possibilities of Social Dreaming*, Karnac Books, London

Macnab, S & Mantel, J-M. (2005) *The Scent of Oneness*, Lulu Press, Morrisville, NC, USA

Maharshi, R and Godman, D. (1998) *Be as You Are: The Teachings of Sri Ramana Maharshi,* Arkana, Penguin Books, London

Mellor, K. Unifying Meditation (Audio CD), Awakening Network, Australia

Melvyn, R. (2011) *The Lost Writings of Wu Hsin*, Summa Iru Publishing, Boulder, Colorado, USA

Nasagadarta,S. (1973) *I Am That*, The Acorn Press, Durham NC, USA

Nouwen, H. (1975) *Reaching Out*, Doubleday & co, New York, USA

Papaji, (2007) *Wake up and Roar*, Sounds True, Boulder, Colorado, USA

Prendergast, J. Fenner, P. Krystal, S (2003) *The Sacred Mirror*, Paragon House, Minnesota, USA.

Rilke, R M, Kline, A (2015) *The Poetry of Rainer Maria Rilke*, Createspace Independent Publishing

Roberts, M. (1997) *The Man Who Listens to Horses,* Arrow; New Ed edition, London, UK

Roche, L. (2014) *The Radiance Sutras: Sounds True*, Boulder, Colorado, USA

Rohr, R. (2013) *Immortal Diamond: The Search for Our True Self,* Society for Promoting Christian Knowledge, London, UK

Rose, S. https://safire-rose.com/books-and-media/poetry/she-let-go

Rosen, D. (1998) *The Tao of Jung*, Penguin, London, UK

Shakespeare, W (1986) *William Shakespeare – The Complete Works* Oxford University Press, Oxford, UK

Shelley, P. Leader, Z. (2009) *The Major Works*, Oxford University Press, Oxford UK

Thich Nhat Hanh, (1993) *Transformation and Healing*, Rider, Ebury Press, London, UK

Tolle, E. (2003) *Stillness Speaks*, New World library, California, USA and Namaste Publishing, Vancouver, Canada

Welwood, J. (2002) *Towards a Psychology of Awakening*, Shambala Publications, Boulder Colorado, USA

Whyte, D. (2015) *Consolations*, Many Rivers Press Langley, Washington, USA

Wilhem, R. (1951) *I Ching, Book of Changes*, Routledge & Kegan Paul, London, UK

Williams, M. and Penman, D. (2011) *Mindfulness: A Practical Guide to Finding Peace in a Frantic World,* Piatkus, London, UK

Appendix: Web based resources

https://mantel.pro – Dr Jean-Marc Mantel's website with many articles and interviews on non-duality.

http://www.nondualtraining.com/ –information about training with Dr Peter Fenner in non-duality and psychotherapy, counselling and coaching and other resources.

http://itaaworld.org/ and https://www.uktransactionalanalysis.co.uk – the international and national websites for Transactional Analysis training, lists of therapists and conferences.

https://www.non-dualmindfulness.com – the author's own website with information about retreats, meetings and supervision.

MANTRA
BOOKS

EASTERN RELIGION & PHILOSOPHY

We publish books on Eastern religions and philosophies. Books
that aim to inform and explore the various traditions that began in
the East and have migrated West.
If you have enjoyed this book, why not tell other readers by
posting a review on your preferred book site.

Recent bestsellers from MANTRA BOOKS are:

The Way Things Are
A Living Approach to Buddhism
Lama Ole Nydahl
An introduction to the teachings of the Buddha, and how to make use of these teachings in everyday life.
Paperback: 978-1-84694-042-2 ebook: 978-1-78099-845-9

Back to the Truth
5000 Years of Advaita
Dennis Waite
A demystifying guide to Advaita for both those new to, and those familiar with this ancient, non-dualist philosophy from India.
Paperback: 978-1-90504-761-1 ebook: 978-184694-624-0

Shinto: A celebration of Life
Aidan Rankin
Introducing a gentle but powerful spiritual pathway reconnecting humanity with Great Nature and affirming all aspects of life.
Paperback: 978-1-84694-438-3 ebook: 978-1-84694-738-4

In the Light of Meditation
Mike George
A comprehensive introduction to the practice of meditation and the spiritual principles behind it. A 10 lesson meditation programme with CD and internet support.
Paperback: 978-1-90381-661-5

A Path of Joy
Popping into Freedom
Paramananda Ishaya
A simple and joyful path to spiritual enlightenment.
Paperback: 978-1-78279-323-6 ebook: 978-1-78279-322-9

The Less Dust the More Trust
Participating in The Shamatha Project, Meditation and Science
Adeline van Waning, MD PhD
The inside-story of a woman participating in frontline meditation research, exploring the interfaces of mind-practice, science and psychology.
Paperback: 978-1-78099-948-7 ebook: 978-1-78279-657-2

I Know How To Live, I Know How To Die
The Teachings of Dadi Janki: A warm, radical, and life-affirming view of who we are, where we come from, and what time is calling us to do
Neville Hodgkinson
Life and death are explored in the context of frontier science and deep soul awareness.
Paperback: 978-1-78535-013-9 ebook: 978-1-78535-014-6

Living Jainism
An Ethical Science
Aidan Rankin, Kanti V. Mardia
A radical new perspective on science rooted in intuitive awareness and deductive reasoning.
Paperback: 978-1-78099-912-8 ebook: 978-1-78099-911-1

Ordinary Women, Extraordinary Wisdom
The Feminine Face of Awakening
Rita Marie Robinson
A collection of intimate conversations with female spiritual teachers who live like ordinary women, but are engaged with their true natures.
Paperback: 978-1-84694-068-2 ebook: 978-1-78099-908-1

The Way of Nothing
Nothing in the Way
Paramananda Ishaya
A fresh and light-hearted exploration of the amazing reality of
nothingness.
Paperback: 978-1-78279-307-6 ebook: 978-1-78099-840-4

Readers of ebooks can buy or view any of these bestsellers by
clicking on the live link in the title. Most titles are published in
paperback and as an ebook. Paperbacks are available in traditional
bookshops. Both print and ebook formats are available online.

Find more titles and sign up to our readers' newsletter at
http://www.johnhuntpublishing.com/mind-body-spirit.
Follow us on Facebook at https://www.facebook.com/OBooks
and Twitter at https://twitter.com/obooks.